DEVON DERBIES
1920-2001

Top left: Plymouth Argyle are known as the Pilgrims, in honour of the city's historical connections with the early American colonists. Top right: In common with other clubs, Torquay United's early black-and-white strip earned them the title of the Magpies. Bottom left: Torquay United changed colours in the mid-1950s, and in 1977 adopted Gulliver as their mascot when they became the Gulls. Bottom right: Exeter City have one of the most unusual nicknames in football. For reasons lost in the mists of time, they have always been dubbed the Grecians.

DEVON DERBIES
1920-2001

Mike Holgate

TEMPUS

First published 2001

PUBLISHED IN THE UNITED KINGDOM BY:

Tempus Publishing Ltd
The Mill, Brimscombe Port
Stroud, Gloucestershire GL5 2QG

PUBLISHED IN THE UNITED STATES OF AMERICA BY:

Tempus Publishing Inc.
2A Cumberland Street
Charleston, SC 29401

Tempus books are available in France and Germany
from the following addresses:

Tempus Publishing Group	Tempus Publishing Group
21 Avenue de la République	Gustav-Adolf-Straße 3
37300 Joué-lès-Tours	99084 Erfurt
FRANCE	GERMANY

British Library Cataloguing in Publication Data.
A catalogue record for this book is available from the British Library.

ISBN 0 7524 1898 X

Typesetting and origination by Tempus Publishing.
PRINTED AND BOUND IN GREAT BRITAIN.

CONTENTS

Plainmoor, April Fools Day 1995. Torquay United and Exeter City exchanged strips and ran out in the colours of their rivals before their home League games. At the end of the day, the joke was on them as both teams lost!

A partisan spectator watches a League encounter between Torquay and Exeter at Plainmoor in February 2000.

INTRODUCTION

Amazingly, since Torquay United joined Plymouth Argyle and Exeter City in the Football League in 1927, the three clubs have spent only twelve seasons in the same division. However, the clubs' yo-yo existence in the lower reaches of the League seems to have come to a shuddering halt as the 2001/2002 campaign will be a record fifth consecutive season for League derbies involving the Pilgrims, the Grecians and the Gulls. This in itself is nothing short of miraculous as Exeter City and Torquay United both finished propping up Division Three during the 1990s and preserved their position in the League on a dubious technicality as the grounds of their designated non-League replacements were deemed sub-standard.

Midway through last season the Devon clubs were in crisis, occupying three of the bottom five places. Argyle were unbeaten by their local rivals which eased their worries, but as the campaign deteriorated for Exeter and Torquay, supporters braced themselves for the worst and clung to the possibility of fate intervening yet again as Carlisle considered defecting to the Scottish League, Chesterfield faced possible expulsion over charges of financial irregularities and amalgamation was proposed between Wimbledon and Crystal Palace. Fortunately, the local sides saved themselves where it matters – on the field of play – although it was a desperately close-run thing, as Torquay left it to the very last game of the season to beat Barnet and condemn their North London opponents to the 'Big Drop'.

With long-term survival in mind, the thorny question of a merger was raised in a 1999 article in the *Herald Express*. The notion of the three clubs becoming 'Devon United' before one or more drop through the trapdoor to non-League oblivion would doubtless meet with strong opposition from club officials and supporters alike, but surely miracles are running out as the expectations of Devon's soccer clubs have now sunk so low that success is measured simply by retaining their League status. Looking on the bright side of this situation, when promotion hopes have been dashed, relegation fears averted, cup runs ended abruptly, the best is yet to come – Devon Derbies!

Mike Holgate
June 2001

ACKNOWLEDGEMENTS

This book would not have been possible without access to contemporary reports in the *Western Morning Mercury*, *Western Morning News*, *Sunday Independent*, *Express & Echo*, *Evening Herald*, *Torquay Times*, *Torquay Directory* and *Herald Express*. These newspapers were kindly made available to me at Torquay Reference Library, Plymouth City Library and the West Country Studies Library, Exeter. Gathering illustrations has involved generous assistance from many sources, and I would like to express my sincere thanks to the following people: fellow *Images of Sport* authors – Dave Fisher, *Exeter City FC 1904-1994*; Gordon Sparks, *Plymouth Argyle 1886-1986*; Ray Simpson, *Burnley FC 1886-1968*; Norman Shiel, *Final Tie: Interwar FA Cup Finals*; Steve Porter of the *Sunday Independent*; Paul Levie of Torbay News Agency; Tony Carney of Acme Photographic Agency; David Mason, chairman of Torbay Postcard Club; Peter Darke and Pete Wilkey. Statistical information has been collated with information from Leigh Edwards, Phil Hollow, Lee Jackson, Wendy Harvey and use of the following reference works: *PFA Premier & Football Player's Records 1946-1998*, edited and compiled by Barry J. Hugman; *Rothmans Football League Yearbooks*; *Plymouth Argyle: A Complete Record 1903-1989* by Brian Knight; *Exeter City FC: A Complete Record 1904-1990* by Maurice Golesworthy; *The Definitive Torquay United*, produced in 1997 by Leigh Edwards. Finally, thanks are due to sports editor James Howarth for affording me the opportunity to pursue my idea for this project.

Mike Holgate
June 2001

1

LEAGUE TUSSLES

The wounded are carried from the field of battle during the Boxing Day derby between Exeter City and Torquay United in 1984.

PLYMOUTH ARGYLE 0 EXETER CITY 0
Third Division, 25 December 1920
(Attendance 18,000)

Argyle (2-3-5): Fred Craig; Moses Russell, Billy Forbes; Jimmy Logan, Jack Hill, Jimmy Dickinson; Patsy Corcoran, Tommy Gallogley, George Sheffield, Harry Raymond, Bert Bowler; Manager: Robert Jack.
City (2-3-5): Dick Pym: Joe Coleburne, John Feebury; Bill Crawshaw, Jim Carrick, Jasper Green; Len Appleton, Jim Makin, Bob Shields, Charlie Vowles, John Dockray; Manager: Arthur Chadwick.

Devon soccer fans flocked to Home Park on Christmas Day 1920 to witness the eagerly awaited inaugural League derby between Plymouth Argyle and Exeter City. As part of the Football League's expansion plans, the two clubs had stepped up from the Southern League to become founder members of the Third Division. This development persuaded Plymouth & District League rivals Torquay Town and Babbacombe to amalgamate and turn professional under the name Torquay United. The Magpies' hopes of emulating Argyle and City came to fruition when they were admitted to the Football League in 1927.

Exeter goalkeeper Dick Pym emerged as the star of this festive encounter and was largely responsible for ensuring the match ended in stalemate. The Grecians kicked off in enterprising fashion and created numerous chances in the first half, although the attack floundered in front of goal as the forwards were guilty of some wayward shooting. Former Huddersfield Town centre forward Bob Shields, making his debut for City, might have had a hat-trick before Argyle 'keeper Fred Craig left the field at half-time somewhat fortunate to have maintained a clean sheet. The Pilgims were a different proposition after the interval and bombarded the visitors' goal, where the agile Dick Pym distinguished himself with a string of brilliant saves. He also had luck on his side when defender Jack Hill headed inches wide, Bert Bowler and Tommy Gallogley each shot over the crossbar from close range and George Sheffield struck the upright with the goal at his mercy. The crowd's frustration grew and their anger was increasingly directed at the referee, who made his presence felt with some strange decisions and was booed off the pitch after sounding the final whistle.

Two days later, the return at St James Park once again ended all-square but produced two goals, with Argyle securing their twelfth draw of the season. There was only one change in the teams with Argyle bringing in veteran Septimus Atterbury to replace full-back Billy Forbes. Striker Bob Shields made up for his poor performance in the previous game and showed what he was capable of by heading City into a first-half lead from a John Dockray cross. Midway through the second half, the home side looked certain to increase their lead but were denied by a fantastic double-save by Fred Craig. The 'keeper palmed down a fierce drive from Charlie Vowles then recovered quickly to fling himself full-length to turn away a pile-driver from John Dockray as the winger latched onto the rebound. The

Left: *Dick Pym, who kept the Argyle attack at bay.* Right: *Moses Russell, who scored a penalty in the return at St James Park.*

Pilgrims snatched an equaliser late in the game when Jasper Green handled on the line in a goalmouth melee and conceded a penalty. Welsh international Moses Russell stepped up to place his spot-kick wide of Dick Pym and the Christmas double ended with honours even.

Plymouth Argyle became the county's first professional football club in 1903. Exeter City followed suit five years later, and The Grecians won the first Devon derby in a Southern League match. Since then, the two clubs have been the keenest of rivals. They have met in the Football League on 54 occasions with Argyle gaining 21 wins to City's 14, and the other 19 matches resulting in a draw. When The Pilgrims won promotion in 1930, the main focus switched to the encounters between Exeter City and Torquay United, who turned professional in 1921. In 94 League encounters, City have won 36, United 29, with 29 matches drawn. Plymouth and Torquay have only met in the same division during 15 seasons, so for many years their derbies did not arouse quite the same passion among supporters, but with The Pilgrims' progress going into decline in the 1990s, this attitude has changed dramatically. Of the 30 League games played, Argyle have won 17, and United 5, with 8 matches drawn.

TORQUAY UNITED 1 EXETER CITY 1
Third Division (South), 27 August 1927
(Attendance 10,749)

United (2-3-5): Laurie Milson; George Cook, George Smith; Maurice Wellock, Frank Wragge, Jack Connor; Jim Mackey, Bert Turner, Jimmy Jones, Tom McGovern, Dan Thompson; Manager: Percy Mackrill.
City (2-3-5): Tom Wainwright; Wilf Lowton, Stan Charlton; Jock Ditchburn, Alex Pool, Henry Warren; George Purcell, Billy McDevitt, Wilf Lievesley, Billy Vaughan, Bob Kirk; Manager: Fred Mavin.

Champions of the Southern League Western Section, Torquay United, gained election to the Football League and for their first fixture in the Third Division (South) the 'babes' of the League were awarded a home derby against Exeter City. There was a carnival atmosphere at Plainmoor, where the crowd were entertained before the match by a Charlie Chaplin impersonator. The Grecians added a nice touch by handing out a souvenir wishing the newcomers luck. Fourteen new players had been signed to bolster United's League campaign and their player-manager, Percy Mackrill, was one of only two members of the Southern League squad to line up for this inaugural match. The other was reserve goalkeeper Laurie Milson, called up at the last minute to replace former England amateur international Archie Bayes, who had suffered an injury in training.

The good-natured supporters of both teams mingled on the terraces and were treated to a highly entertaining game played in an excellent spirit.

Exeter 'keeper Tom Wainwright turns the ball over the bar.

Midway through the first half, City full-back Wilf Lowton handled a cross from winger Dan Thompson. Inside forward Bert Turner made no mistake from the spot-kick and earned the distinction of scoring United's first League goal. Within a minute of the restart, Wilf Lowton had the opportunity to make amends for his earlier indiscretion but thudded a penalty against the crossbar after full-back George Smith had also been penalised for handball.

Torquay clung onto their lead until the interval, but Exeter dominated the second half. Laurie Milson emerged as the Man of the Match with a string of brilliant saves to deny the City attack. Just when it seemed the home side would collect both points, City's persistence finally paid off four minutes from the end. The move which led to the equaliser was started by Wilf Lowton, who atoned for his earlier errors by playing a long ball up the wing to George Purcell. The winger's cross was cleverly held up by centre forward Wilf Lievesley, then released into the path of Billy Vaughan whose low drive bounced awkwardly to beat the 'keeper's outstretched hand. With seconds remaining, United had a glorious chance to regain the lead when right-half Maurice Wellock found Bert Turner with a through-ball, but his shot was smartly saved at the foot of the post by 'keeper Tom Wainwright.

Torquay's League debut had been satisfactory, but they were in for a rude awakening. Two days later, they travelled to Millwall and were mauled 9-1 at The Den. United ended a disappointing season at the bottom of the table with only 30 points from 42 matches. Obliged to apply for re-election, they fortunately gained enough votes from other clubs to retain their League status.

TORQUAY UNITED 3 PLYMOUTH ARGYLE 4
Third Division (South), 4 September 1929
(Attendance 8,299)

United (2-3-5): Harold Gough; Frank Womack (player-manager), Jack Fowler; Syd Cann, Harry Bruce, Bob Smith; Jack Burn, Harry Rice, Joe Hill, Harry Keeling, Andy Martin; Manager: Frank Womack.
Argyle (2-3-5): Fred Craig; Harry Bland, Freddie Titmus; Norman Mackay, Fred McKenzie, Alec Hardie; Alf Matthews, Frank Sloan, Ray Bowden, Jack Leslie, Sammy Black; Manager: Robert Jack.

This seven-goal thriller at Plainmoor produced one of the greatest derby matches ever played between the two clubs. Since their election to the Third Division (South), Torquay had failed to beat Plymouth in four League meetings and the first half gave no indication of how hard the Pilgrims would have to work to keep up their unbeaten record against the team then dubbed the Magpies.

Argyle soaked up early pressure from the home side then struck back to open up a two-goal lead from set pieces. The immortal Sammy Black created both chances with accurate left-wing corners. After twenty-four minutes, the first flag kick was headed past former England 'keeper, Harold Gough, by an international centre forward of the future, Ray Bowden. The second cross was also met with a firm header by Sammy's inside partner Jack Leslie. To the delight of the home fans, a dramatic turn-around occurred in the second half as United made light work of the two-goal deficit. Five minutes after the break, centre forward Joe Hill pulled one back when he out-jumped the defence to head in a left-wing cross from Andy Martin. Two minutes later, the fourth headed goal of the match levelled the scores, when Harry Keeling neatly glanced in a right-wing cross.

With the visitors' defence reeling, United kept on the attack and, unbelievably, took the lead after sixty-seven minutes when Keeling was put through by Jack Burn, and scored his second goal with a shot on the run from an oblique angle. The ecstatic cheers of the crowd had still not died down when Argyle were immediately offered a lifeline. Sammy Black cut inside the box and was brought down by United player-manager, Frank Womack. The crowd fell silent as Plymouth 'keeper Fred Craig took the long walk from his own penalty area, calmly placed the ball on the spot, and then deceived his counterpart to bring Argyle back into the match. Three minutes later, a remarkable passage of play ended with yet another chance made by the unstoppable Sammy Black. The winger tormented the United defence before hitting a cross-field pass which was well controlled by right-winger Alf Matthews before he slammed in the winner.

This was only the second match of the season, leaving United at the bottom of the table and Argyle in third place. By the end of the League campaign, both teams had improved their positions. United climbed to fifth from bottom and Argyle emerged as champions. The Pilgrims had endured a record six consecutive seasons as runners-up during the 1920s – when only the top club was

Penalty expert Fred Craig.

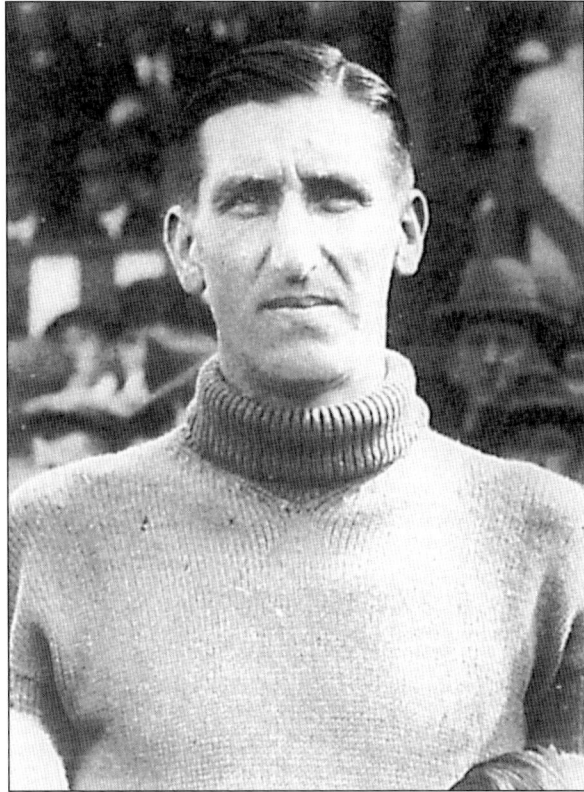

promoted – but to the delight of all Devon soccer fans, they finally booked their passage into the Second Division. Plymouth's success meant that it would be twenty years before the three Devon clubs were reunited in League competition.

Argyle emerged as front-runners for promotion during the 1920s, and completed their first double over City, with emphatic back-to-back 4-0 victories on Christmas Day and Boxing Day 1923! The Pilgrims accomplished this festive feat again in 1926, before The Grecians reversed the trend and gained their first double over their arch rivals the following season. Exeter romped to their first double over Torquay in 1933, and United did not return the favour until 1954. Argyle have completed the double five times over Torquay, since achieving it at the first attempt in 1927. United had to wait until 1971 to give The Greens a double dose of their own medicine, but Argyle quickly shook off the symptoms and, so far, The Gulls have been unable to administer similar treatment!

TORQUAY UNITED 2 EXETER CITY 1
Third Division (South), 28 December 1946
(Attendance 11,500)

United (2-3-5): Gerry Matier: Albert 'Bob' Keeton, Ralph Calland; Bill Towers, Bert Head, Dave Pryde; Russell Phillips, Bill Harrower, Jack Conley, Harry Cothliffe, Dave Mercer; Manager: Jack Butler.
City (2-3-5): Barney Singleton; George Thompson, John Blood; Stan Cutting, Harry Hanford, Steve Walker; Trevor Granville, Bill Fellowes, Harry Holman, Arthur Hydes, Doug Regan; Manager: George Roughton.

Exeter City and Torquay United were pitched into a derby on the opening day of the first post-war League season, which ended with honours even in a 1-1 draw at St James Park. The return fixture came in the aftermath of Christmas Day games, in which City had shown the more convincing away form, beating Brighton 6-1, whilst United had been thrashed by the same score at Crystal Palace. Both Devon clubs had won their Boxing Day returns against the same opposition by the odd goal in three. The derby day crowd was the largest seen

Exeter's Stan Cutting covers Jack Conley on the line, as 'keeper Barney Singleton and full-back George Thompson race out to clear the danger.

for a match at Plainmoor, beating the record set on the Magpies' League debut against Exeter in 1927.

Exeter had eleven players on the injured list, including Christmas Day hat-trick hero, Bill Owen. Their reshuffled side fell behind after ten minutes when Dave Mercer was put through on the left and crossed to the far post, where his fellow winger Russell Phillips scored with a low, crisp shot from close range. The action was fast and furious and both goalkeepers were kept on their toes. Torquay's midfield general, Bill Harrower, demonstrated the skill which would later make the young Scot a favourite at St James Park. His prompting and service to the wings posed a constant threat to the Grecians' defence, and they were fortunate to escape further punishment when centre forward Jack Conley headed against the bar, and a shot from Harry Cothliffe struck the upright. Injuries to wingers Phillips and Mercer reduced United's cutting edge and just before the interval, City snatched an equaliser through an own goal. Centre half Bert Head unluckily deflected a cross from winger Doug Regan past 'keeper Gerry Matier. The visitors pressed hard after the break, and Matier was called into action to save a long-range drive from wing-half Steve Walker. The deciding goal came in the fifty-third minute, when Jack Conley enhanced his reputation as the best header of a ball ever seen in a United shirt. Full-back Ralph Calland floated over a long ball from the left, and the striker rose above the defence to give 'keeper Barney Singleton no chance with a superb header which flew in at the near post

Play deteriorated for the remainder of the game with both trainers much in evidence, administering the 'magic sponge' to the walking wounded – who were forced to continue, as substitutes would not be introduced for another twenty years. Russell Phillips was forced to leave the field temporarily with a pulled muscle and his marker, full-back John Blood, was also hurt but recovered after attention. Late in the game, the Grecians missed a great opportunity to grab a point. Doug Regan seemed certain to level the scores when he outstripped the defence, only to lose out to Gerry Matier who raced off his line and dived bravely at the forward's feet to smother the ball.

PLYMOUTH ARGYLE 2 TORQUAY UNITED 2
Third Division (South), 26 April 1952
(Attendance 28,728)

Argyle (2-3-5): Bill Shortt; Paddy Ratcliffe, Pat Jones; Tony McShane, Jack Chisholm, John Porteous; Gordon Astall, George Dews, Maurice Tadman, Peter Rattray, Alex Govan; Manager: Jimmy Rae.
United (2-3-5): George Webber; Dave Topping, Albert Stitfall; Dennis Lewis, Eric Webber (player-manager), Bill Towers; Ron Shaw, Marwood Marchant, Tommy Northcott, Ernie Edds, Billy Thomas.

Sportingly, Torquay United players formed a guard of honour as Argyle skipper, Jumbo Chisholm, clutching a green and white umbrella, led his team of promotion heroes onto the pitch to a rapturous welcome from the huge Home Park crowd. The championship of the Third Division (South) had been secured with an away win in the previous game at Brighton. In normal circumstances, the result of their last home game might have been considered academic, however, derby pride was at stake against a Torquay side which had defeated them in the corresponding fixture at Plainmoor.

Torquay did their level best to spoil the party. For the first half-hour, the occasion seemed to have completely overwhelmed Argyle as United stormed into a two-goal lead. After fourteen minutes, winger Ron Shaw was put through by Tommy Northcott to beat Welsh international 'keeper Bill Shortt with a 20-yard pile-driver. Former Argyle forward, Ernie Edds, added the second when he seized on a miskicked clearance by Tony McShane. Moments later, Billy Thomas bundled the ball into the net during a goalmouth scramble, and Argyle fans breathed a sigh of relief as the goal was disallowed for handball. This incident proved to be the turning point of the match, for within five minutes the Pilgrims pulled one back when 'Gentleman George' Dews collected his 25th goal of the season – before resuming his cricket career with Worcestershire CCC. Before the interval, United had chances to regain a two-goal cushion. Bill Shortt proved equal to the danger however, saving a header from Edds, then diving to punch out a powerful drive from Shaw.

Plymouth were fully focused on the job in hand when they took to the field after the interval. It was Torquay's turn to defend desperately and 'keeper George Webber, who earlier had rarely been troubled, was called into action to make several fine saves. Midway through the second half, the inevitable equaliser came from Argyle's top scorer, Maurice Tadman. Peter Rattray crossed the ball from the left, Dews cleverly hooked it over his head and Tadman smashed in his 27th goal of the season from the edge of the area. It was Argyle's 107th goal of the current campaign, which equalled the highest number of goals scored in the club's history.

Argyle finished the match in style, and their fighting recovery might have secured both points. Appeals for handball were turned down by the referee

Torquay United players sportingly applaud Plymouth Argyle, as they are led on to the pitch by skipper 'Jumbo' Chisholm.

when winger Alex Govan slammed the ball against a wall of defenders in the penalty area. The best opportunity to clinch the game fell to the irrepressible Tadman just before the close. The goal-hungry striker hit a powerful drive, which was brilliantly tipped over the bar by Webber. Plymouth finished the season having lost only once at Home Park. Torquay had the consolation of being the only team in the division to emerge unbeaten home and away by the champions.

Since Exeter City and Plymouth Argyle were joined in the Football League by Torquay United in 1927, the three clubs have spent only thirteen years in the same division. These were the seasons beginning in 1927, 1928, 1929, 1950, 1951, 1956, 1957, 1995, 1997, 1998, 1999, 2000 and 2001. The campaign starting in the year 2001 is the first time the clubs have spent five consecutive seasons lining up against each other in the League. Similarly, following the addition of the Fourth Division in 1958, there have been no League derbies during the nine years the clubs spent in three separate divisions. These were the seasons beginning in 1960, 1961, 1964, 1965, 1966, 1967, 1986, 1990 and 1991.

TORQUAY UNITED 1 PLYMOUTH ARGYLE 1
Third Division (South), 23 March 1957
(Attendance 12,038)

United (2-3-5): Mervyn Gill; John Smith, Harry Smith; Denis Lewis, Griff Norman, Norman 'Nobby' Clarke; Graham Bond, Sam Collins, Harold Dobbie, Don Mills, Tony Collins; Manager: Eric Webber.
Argyle (2-3-5): Harry Brown; George Robertson, Pat Jones; Johnny Williams, Peter Langman, Rex Tilley; George Baker, Neil Dougall, Neil Langman, Jack Rowley (player-manager), Peter Anderson.

Before this derby, Plymouth Argyle had not scored in their three previous games and were struggling to stay out of the bottom six. They visited Plainmoor, where United were unbeaten and had not dropped a point at home for four months, as they mounted their first serious bid for promotion. Torquay had already knocked Argyle out of the FA Cup and gained a point at Home Park, without conceding a goal in either game. They came into this third meeting hoping for two points to close the gap on front-runners Ipswich Town and Colchester United.

Danger man Don Mills was an instant target for the Argyle defenders, who

Torquay forward Howard Dobbie is foiled by former Argyle team-mate Harry Brown, while full-back Pat Jones looks on.

conceded early free-kicks for some crude tackles. The midfield general shook off the close attention of his markers to go close with a header that thudded against the crossbar. Although not renowned for his ability in the air, he went one better with his next attempt. After half an hour, winger Tony Collins swung in a corner from the left and 'The Don' rose magnificently to beat Harry Brown's despairing dive. This was the highlight of a poor first half, and United went into the interval holding onto their slender lead.

Argyle came out fighting and set a storming pace after the break, but produced little evidence to suggest that they could end their goal drought. They dominated play and had the United defence struggling, but lacked bite in front of goal. When the equaliser came after sixty-five minutes, it was a complete fluke and cruel luck for the home team. United skipper Dennis Lewis attempted to hook the ball away from the goalmouth. The clearance struck Neil Langman full in the face and flew past 'keeper Mervyn Gill. The stunned striker knew nothing about it, he just happened to be standing in the right place at the right time. Argyle, encouraged by this good fortune, went all out for the winner against their demoralised opponents, and Gill was called upon to make fine saves to deny Johnny Williams and Neil Dougall. With time running out, United had a wonderful opportunity to regain the lead with a counter attack which put Don Mills through with only Harry Brown to beat, but his powerful left-foot drive cleared the bar.

In the final analysis, this sacrificed point cost United dear. They went into the last match of the season at Crystal Palace requiring a win to fulfil their promotion aspirations. The result was a disappointing draw, which gave them the same number of points as Ipswich, who were crowned champions with a superior goal average. It was the first management success of Alf Ramsey who took Town to the old First Division championship, before guiding England to victory in the 1966 World Cup. Torquay would never again come so close to reaching the upper echelons of the Football League!

Many young players had to put their soccer careers on hold during the Second World War and were reaching the veteran stage before peace and League soccer were restored. Future Plymouth and Exeter manager Ellis Stuttard made a single appearance for Argyle in 1939 at the age of nineteen, and waited until 1946 before adding to the total. He joined Torquay in 1948, and there partnered full-back Ralph Calland, who had a similar experience. Signed by Charlton as a twenty-one-year-old in 1937, he failed to make the first team and was transferred to United two years later. The outbreak of war meant that he was unable to make his League debut until the age of thirty! Despite this setback, Ralph made over 200 appearances for United and ran the 'A' team for many years after his playing days were over.

TORQUAY UNITED 2 EXETER CITY 3
Fourth Division, 26 December 1959
(Attendance 10,231)

United (2-3-5): Mervyn Gill; John Smith, Dennis Penford; Colin Bettany, George Northcott, Colin Rawson; Larry Baxter, Geoff Cox, Tommy Northcott, Graham Bond, Don Mills; Manager: Eric Webber.
City (2-3-5): Alan Jones; Theo Foley, Les MacDonald; Arnold Mitchell, Ken Oliver, Jim Thompson; Nelson Stiffle, Graham Rees, Jack Wilkinson, Andy Micklewright, Gordon Dale; Manager: Frank Broome.

Torquay United came into this Boxing Day derby clinging onto second place in the table, despite losing their last two home games. Exeter City were fast-improving after an indifferent start to the campaign. Having won their last two away games, the Grecians obviously relished the prospect of repeating their success of the previous season, when they had won a thrilling match at Plainmoor by the odd goal in seven.

Both sides ploughed through the mud to create several chances in the first half. United's most dangerous forward, Geoff Cox, created a great

Graham Rees notched City's second goal.

chance which was fired just wide by centre forward Tommy Northcott, then went close himself with two headers. The second effort, from a long Don Mills cross, was brilliantly turned around the post by 'keeper Alan Jones. Exeter gradually gained the upper hand as they adapted to the glue-pot conditions. With wingers Nelson Stiffle and Gordon Dale revelling in the firmer ground on the flanks, the City attack began to put the home defence under increasing pressure – which produced an amazing seventeen corners before half-time. The last one was awarded three minutes before the break, and Dale's flag-kick was converted in a goalmouth scramble by centre forward Jack Wilkinson. City extended their lead further, soon after the interval, when inside right Graham Rees ran onto a defence-splitting pass from Nelson Stiffle and chipped over advancing 'keeper Mervyn Gill from the edge of the area.

United had started with Don Mills playing out of position on the left wing. Midway through the second half, he reverted to his normal midfield role by switching with Graham Bond and the tactical move paid immediate dividends. Geoff Cox latched onto a Mills through ball and reduced the arrears with a superb long-range strike. With ten minutes to go, Nelson Stiffle capped a fine display by restoring Exeter's two-goal lead. In a late rally, Tommy Northcott lost his marker, Ken Oliver, to meet a Graham Bond cross and grab a second goal for United. This was, however, only a consolation goal for a United side who were flattered by the final score.

Despite this reversal, United journeyed to St James for the return two days later in confident mood, having won 8 and lost only 3 of their 11 away matches that season. However, their promotion hopes suffered another setback when City completed the double over their neighbours with the only goal of the game. Torquay may have lost the derby battle, but they were still in the war. During the remainder of the season, they dropped only one more point at home as they finished in third place. This tremendous run-in gained them promotion for the first time in their history.

TORQUAY UNITED 1 EXETER CITY 1
Fourth Division, 30 March 1964
(Attendance 13,655)

United (2-3-5): Terry Adlington; John Williams, George Allen; Ray Spencer, Colin Bettany, Trevor Wolstenholme; Peter Anderson, Robin Stubbs, Brian Handley, Reg Jenkins, Ernie Pym; Manager: Eric Webber.
City (2-3-5): Alan Barnett; Cecil Smyth, Les MacDonald; Dave Hancock, Keith Harvey, Des Anderson; Graham Rees, Alan Banks, Dermot Curtis, Derek Grace, Adrian Thorne; Manager: Jack Edwards.

This Easter Monday derby had an extra edge, as both teams had promotion aspirations. Exeter City were well placed, five points ahead of Torquay United who had two games in hand on their rivals. At St James Park on Good Friday, United had 'drawn' first blood by gaining an important away point in a scrappy, scoreless stalemate. Undaunted by this poor display, the fans flocked to Plainmoor to see if either side could gain the upper hand in the return. Most of the thrills, both of the goals, and by far the best football were seen in the first half. The only highlight after this promising start was a troupe of eight can-can dancers who enlivened the interval with their performance, before the game dragged out to another tame draw.

United's leading marksman, Robin Stubbs, had been unfit for the first derby encounter, but made his comeback in this match and immediately made his presence felt. Turning out with a heavily-strapped thigh, he lashed a shot against the post after thirty seconds as United mounted an all-out attack. Centre forward Brian Handley also went close with two headers, before City broke out of defence to snatch a fourteenth minute lead. Striker Alan Banks took a through-pass from winger Graham Rees, and curled in a cross for Eire international Dermot Curtis to beat 'keeper Terry Adlington with a superb diving header. City 'keeper Alan Barnett saved well from Brian Handley and Reg Jenkins before United equalised after twenty-eight minutes. Good work by former Argyle winger, Peter Anderson, set up Brian Handley, whose hard drive was deflected on its way into the net by full-back Cec Smyth. United winger Ernie Pym had a goal disallowed and a shot from Handley was well cleared by full-back Les MacDonald, as the City defence withstood the bombardment until the interval.

Torquay's forwards simply wore themselves out in the second half trying to penetrate Exeter's ironclad defence system. During the game, Exeter did not win a single corner, while United were awarded sixteen but could not turn them into material advantage. Late in the game, the home team finally prised open Exeter's bastion and had two good opportunities to win the match. Both chances fell to Ernie Pymm, but his two attempts flew well wide of the target. Mission accomplished, the visitors left the field well satisfied with a point and emerged at the end of the season clinging onto the all-important fourth and final promotion place. While the Grecians were celebrating their first taste of tangible League success, Torquay were left trailing in their wake finishing two places behind their neighbours. It would be another two

Terry Adlington saves from the feet of striker Alan Banks, while defender Colin Bettany covers.

seasons before United moved up to the Third Division. Unfortunately, the resumption of derby hostilities had to be put on hold as City were simultaneously sliding back in the opposite direction to the Fourth Division!

Exeter and Torquay played an April Fool's Day joke on their supporters in 1995, when they ran out for the kick-about before their home games wearing their arch-rivals' team strip. The joke was on them however, when they both lost their League matches! In April 1948, Torquay United did not have a fit goalkeeper on the books and pressed reserve half-back John Casley into service for a crucial end of season League encounter against Walsall. John played a 'blinder' between the posts in a thrilling 3-2 victory, which ensured that United avoided finishing bottom of the League. The unassuming hero was carried shoulder-high from the field by supporters, but this was a brief moment of glory for John, for this would prove to be the only occasion when he appeared in a League match! Similarly, 'keeper Richard Crabtree has the unusual distinction of making a single League appearance for both Torquay and Exeter. He was called upon in April 1976 to play as a non-contract player in United's win over Workington, then waited eight years for his next League game, turning out in the drawn derby between City against Argyle in April 1984!

TORQUAY UNITED 2 PLYMOUTH ARGYLE 1
Third Division, 1 April 1972
(Attendance 10,928)

United (4-3-3): John Connaughton; Clint Boulton, Dick Edwards, Brian W Hill (sub: Ian Twitchin), Dave Stocks; Mal Lucas, Alan Welsh, Bruce Stuckey; Dave Tearse, Robin Stubbs, Cliff Jackson; Manager: Jack Edwards.
Argyle (4-3-3): Peta Balac; Alan Harris, John Hore, Dave Provan, Colin Sullivan; Mickey Cave, Neil Hague, Les Latcham; Ronnie Brown, Jimmy Hinch, Don Hutchins; Manager: Ellis Stuttard.

What a difference a season makes! A year after establishing themselves as Devon's top club by completing their first, and so far only, League double over Argyle, Torquay came into this Easter derby staring relegation in the face at the bottom of the table. Plymouth were on the fringe of the promotion race and, having already beaten the Gulls convincingly at Home Park, were hoping to consolidate their place in the top six with a win at Plainmoor. United's poor performances had already seen the departure of manager Allan Brown, who had made an unfortunate self-fulfilling prophecy: 'This team will get me the sack!'

Argyle got off to a confident start and gave the United defence a thorough workout in the opening ten minutes. Loan 'keeper John Connaughton, making

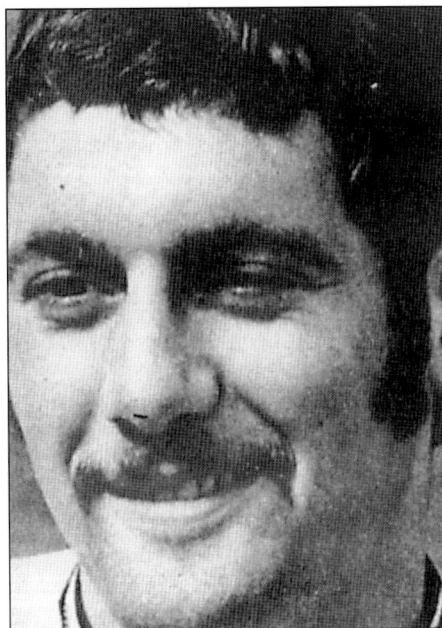

Left: *Former Gull Mickey Cave creates Argyle's goal.* Right: *United's Alan Welsh scores his first goal in five months.*

his last appearance at Torquay before his recall to Manchester United, had to deal with the early threat of Jim Hinch, Don Hutchins and former Gulls' favourite, Mickey Cave. The balance of the match changed dramatically in the eleventh minute, when Alan Welsh scored his first goal for five months. Argyle 'keeper Peta Balac punched out a cross from left-back Dave Stocks, and Welsh powered in one of his rocket-like 'specials' from outside the area. Argyle went close to equalising with a spectacular overhead kick from Neil Hague which shaved the bar, then Connaughton saved well from Mickey Cave. United rode their luck and delivered a hammer-blow to the visitors five minutes before the interval. Plymouth's Player of the Year, Dave Provan, was given the slip by former Argyle winger Cliff Jackson. The resulting cross was slammed past Balac by striker Dave Tearse. Torquay were forced to reshuffle their defence from the restart. Clint Boulton moved to the centre to replace injured Brian W. Hill, with substitute Ian Twitchin slotting in at full-back. The Gulls were hard-pressed at the back as Argyle renewed their efforts to reduce the arrears. John Connaughton moved quickly to clear the danger by punching the ball off the head of Jim Hinch. The striker was thwarted again when a goal-bound effort was headed over the bar by Clint Boulton. Hinch finally got on the score sheet after eighty-two minutes, rising to head home his ninth goal of the season from a Mickey Cave cross.

Despite a tense climax, United hung on for two valuable points which still left them in dire straits at the foot of the table. Argyle's flickering promotion hopes never recovered from this defeat. The Pilgrims' manager, Ellis Stuttard, generously conceded that on this display, Torquay were in a false position and did not deserve to go down. However, this derby victory signalled a temporary revival which proved too little, too late for United. Although they pulled themselves up to second from bottom, above Bradford City, the Gulls lost their relegation battle and were consigned to the basement League, where they were to remain for almost twenty years.

The Football League unveiled the names of '100 League Legends' in August 1998 to commemorate their centennial season. Among the players honoured, were four internationals with connections to Westcountry clubs. David Jack, the Bolton Wanderers, Arsenal and England great, started his League career with Plymouth Argyle in 1920. Playing alongside him for the Gunners was Cliff Bastin, the finest soccer player ever born in Exeter, who left his hometown club to win all the game's major honours before his twenty-first birthday. Two goalkeepers honoured by the Football League turned out for Devon clubs late in their careers. England's most capped international, Peter Shilton, took over as Argyle's player-manager in 1992. Similarly, Neville Southall is Wales' most capped international, and was voted Torquay United's Player of the Year in 1999.

TORQUAY UNITED 0 EXETER CITY 1
Fourth Division, 8 April 1977
(Attendance 7,966)

United (4-3-3): Robbie Robbins; Ian Twitchin, Mike Green (player-manager),
Clint Boulton, Kenny Sandercock; Barry Vassalo, Dave Rudge, Dave Kennedy;
Andy Provan (sub: Steve Morrall), Willie Brown, Colin Lee.
City: (4-3-4): John Baugh; John Templeman, Bobby Saxton (player-manager),
Peter Hatch, John Hore; Bobby Hodge, Lammie Robertson, Graham Weeks;
Alan Beer, Tony Kellow, Nicky Jennings.

This Good Friday derby was a classic confrontation, with Torquay trying to pull
away from the re-election zone and Exeter vying for promotion. Former Argyle
team-mates, Mike Green and Bobby Saxton, were having contrasting experi-
ences in their first taste of management and, for different reasons, they both
hoped desperately for two points from this match.

Exeter City certainly looked the better side by the length of the division in
the first half. United were totally outclassed, and it was no surprise when they
fell behind after twenty-one minutes. Goalkeeper John Baugh made a long
clearance which was touched on by Tony Kellow into the path of his twin striker
Alan Beer. The blistering pace of Beer left United's square defence trailing, as
he ran through to beat onrushing 'keeper Robbie Robbins from 12 yards. This
brilliantly executed 'route one' goal was to prove the winner. The Grecians had

Alan Beer slots the winner past Robbie Robbins.

many opportunities to wrap up the game before the interval, with Robbins doing particularly well to deny Kellow and Beer. Torquay had a gilt-edged chance to equalise ten minutes before the interval, when a mistake by full-back John Hore let in Andy Provan. With the City defence hopelessly exposed, the winger's tame cross failed to reach unmarked forwards Willie Brown and Colin Lee, allowing defender Bobby Saxton to concede a corner gratefully.

A stirring fightback was the very least expected of United by their supporters, and the home team delivered in the second half. Sheer grit and determination appeared to have paid off in the seventy-fourth minute when leading scorer Willie Brown rushed through to plant the ball firmly in the net. Unfortunately for the Gulls, the goal was disallowed as the referee had already blown up for a foul on Barry Vassalo in midfield. Earlier, central defender Clint Boulton had rattled the crossbar with a header following a Vassalo corner. As United battled for a point in the closing minutes, Mike Green had a header and a shot blocked, and further attempts by Colin Lee and Barry Vassalo flew wide of the target.

Exeter completed the double over their neighbours and received a huge boost to their confidence during the run-in at the end of the season. Bobby Saxton's side deservedly achieved promotion by finishing as runners-up behind champions Cambridge United. Malcolm Musgrove, Lew Chatterly and Frank O'Farrell had all taken turns at the helm during Torquay's fluctuating campaign before Mike Green was appointed in charge of team affairs, a month before this crucial derby. He subsequently worked wonders in turning around the club's fortunes. After the defeat by City, the Gulls lost only one of their last nine games and averted the threat of re-election by climbing to mid-table respectability.

EXETER CITY 1 PLYMOUTH ARGYLE 1
Third Division, 21 April 1984
(Attendance 6,870)

City (4-3-3): Richard Crabtree; Graeme Kirkup, Simon Webster, Nicky Marker, Keith Viney; Mark O'Connor, Martin Ling (sub: Frank Howarth), Steve Harrower; John Sims, Ray Pratt, Roy McDonough; Manager: Gerry Francis. Argyle (4-3-3): Geoff Crudgington; Gordon Nisbet, Chris Harrison, Lindsay Smith, John Uzzell; Leigh Cooper, Kevin Hodges, Dave Phillips; Tommy Tynan (sub: Neville Chamberlain), Gordon Staniforth, Andy Rogers; Manager: John Hore.

Argyle's dream of Wembley glory had been ended cruelly, five days before this crucial relegation clash. The Pilgrims had barely had time to recover from their devastating FA Cup semi-final defeat by Watford, before having to concentrate on their precarious League position against desperate derby rivals Exeter, who were firmly rooted to the bottom of the table. Argyle's wonderful cup deeds were not reflected by their League results, and they came into this match knowing that City could drag them down into the relegation mire.

Before the game, St James Park was 'buzzed' by a light aircraft with a message for the home fans from rebel director Dan McCauley, who had been voted off the board after being openly critical of club policy. As the plane circled the ground of the relegation-haunted club, it trailed a banner with a message aimed at club chairman Clifford Hill: 'Without Dan, it's down Hill.'

The pre-match entertainment over, the business of the day started in earnest. The game got off to a sensational start in the first minute when Exeter skipper Keith Viney went on an overlapping full-back's raid down the left flank, played a one-two with Ray Pratt, then cut in to lash a shot against the upright. Argyle immediately counter-attacked and Exeter defender Nicky Marker made a goal-line clearance to avert the danger. Plymouth gradually gained control and won seven corners in the first half-hour. From one of these flag-kicks, Lindsay Smith got up superbly to head against the post. The Greens' leading scorer, Tommy Tynan, had a goal disallowed for offside before City delivered a shock to the visitors by taking the lead against the run of play. Martin Ling took a quick throw-in to Roy McDonaugh, who caught the defence flat-footed with a deep cross from the right, which found Ray Pratt in space. The striker brilliantly took his chance by hooking the ball over 'keeper Geoff Crudgington. The Grecians tried desperately to cling onto this slender lead and break a run of 17 games without a win. Just when it seemed the home side would hold out, Argyle grabbed a deserved equaliser. Winger Andy Rogers collected the ball from a Crudgington clearance and found substitute Neville Chamberlain. His pinpoint cross was met by Gordon Staniforth to beat City's debutant 'keeper Richard Crabtree with a glancing header.

This result left City stranded on the rocks of certain relegation and kept

'*Keeper Richard Crabtree thwarts the Argyle attack.*

Argyle just two points above the bottom four. Subsequent results took the Pilgrims deep into the danger zone before a late rally salvaged their season as they finished sixth from bottom.

The Football League followed up their '100 League Legends' by asking soccer fans around the country to vote for their favourite 'Local Legend'. The poll was organized by regional newspapers and the results published in 1999. Votes were not cast for the 'Hot 100' already selected, and Devon supporters came out in favour of Paul Mariner, who oozed class for Argyle in the mid-1970s before winning England caps with Ipswich Town; striker Tony Kellow, who scored more goals for Exeter City than any other player during three spells with the club during the 1970s and 1980s; and midfield maestro Don Mills, who first won an army of Torquay United fans while on loan from QPR in 1948, and returned to make the United team tick in the 1950s.

TORQUAY UNITED 1 EXETER CITY 2
Fourth Division, 1 April 1986
(Attendance 2,555)

United (4-4-2): Dave Fry; Derek Fowler, Paul Compton, Steve Wright, Steve Pugh; Dave West, Steve Pyle, Derek Dawkins, Mark Loram; Steve Phillips, Mario Walsh; Manager: Stuart Morgan.
City (4-3-3): John Shaw; Jim McNichol, Aiden McCaffrey, Nicky Marker, Keith Viney; Martin Ling, Danny Keough, Gary Jackson; Tony Kellow, Warren Ward, Steve Harrower; Manager: Colin Appleton.

Before this derby, Torquay had lost only three of their last 13 League games, but still remained adrift at the foot of the table in the face of similar revivals by their fellow strugglers. It seemed that nothing short of a miracle of Biblical proportions could save them from finishing bottom of the table for the second successive season. The Gulls had brought home a point from St James Park four days earlier, after fighting back from being two goals down in the first four minutes, and a win in the return could push Exeter City dangerously close to the re-election zone. The Plainmoor crowd was the lowest ever for a League derby between the sides, yet it was United's highest gate of the season.

The Grecians were by far the brighter side and should have been two or three goals up by half-time. Goalkeeper Dave Fry had to deal with shots from Warren Ward and Gary Jackson, and raced off his line to save from Ward and Tony Kellow. City's best effort came in the fifteenth minute, when Jim McNichol headed a Gary Jackson corner against the near post. Veteran striker Tony Kellow fired wide in the thirty-fourth minute, and Martin Ling and Jim McNichol both had shots blocked before Steve Phillip ended a frustrating half for the visitors with a snap-shot on the turn which flew wide. These misses appeared costly when United were awarded a penalty five minutes after the break. Mark Loram beat Jim McNichol on the left and hoisted a high cross to the far post, where Mario Walsh was pushed by defender Nicky Marker. Steve Phillips hammered the spot-kick past John Shaw to give the Gulls an unconvincing lead.

City stormed back to level within five minutes when Fry stopped, but failed to hold, Jim McNichol's header from a Martin Ling corner. Opportunist Tony Kellow was first to react and toe-poked the ball home from close range. Both sides seemed to have settled for a point until City were presented with all three of them after seventy-seven minutes. Martin Ling cut in from the right wing and hit a weak left-foot shot from 20 yards, which bobbled over the outstretched hand of a mortified Dave Fry.

Exeter's derby victory condemned their neighbours to seek re-election and the Gulls remained rooted to the bottom of the table, winning only one of their remaining nine games. The Grecians seemed to have pulled away from the danger zone, but a string of poor results sucked them back to fourth from bottom. Both clubs successfully applied for re-election, but this was the last time they could rely

Tony Kellow, who snatched City's equaliser.

on the 'old boy' network for their League status. Automatic relegation to the Conference League for the club finishing bottom was introduced the following season. Torquay seemed doomed to finish propping up the League for the third year running, until an injury-time equaliser in the last game of the season against Crewe Alexandra pulled them up to second from bottom on goal difference, saving them from non-League oblivion.

In January 2000, the 'Sunday Independent' produced a special supplement, 'Millennium Moments in Sport', which included Mike Holgate's choice of a Plymouth Argyle Team of the Century:

'This formidable Argyle side features a penalty-taking specialist in goal-keeper Fred Craig, who converted five spot-kicks in the 1920s. In front of him, the back four contains 1960s full-back Tony Book (who went on to lead Manchester City to League and Cup success) and three inter-war internationals: England centre-half Jack Hill and Welsh pair John Pullen and Moses Russell. The midfield general would be the incomparable David Jack, who scored the first FA Cup goal at Wembley for Bolton in 1923, played for Herbert Chapman's great Arsenal side, and was capped for England. Alongside him is Jack Leslie, whose legendary left-wing partnership with Sammy Black, forged in the 1920s, is preserved. On the other flank is Gordon Astall, who appeared in the 1956 FA Cup final with Birmingham and was capped twice on the right wing for England, back in the era of Stanley Matthews and Tom Finney. There is an embarrassment of riches among the strikers, with no room for great goalscorers, Maurice Tadman, Wilf Carter, Jack Cock or Tommy Tynan. My vote goes to a pairing of two England internationals from either side of the war – Ray Bowden and Paul Mariner, who both left Argyle to play at the highest level with Arsenal and Ipswich respectively. Post-war players on the substitutes' bench would be goalkeeper Jim Furnell, swashbuckling centre-back Jack Chisholm, Welsh wing wizard Barry Jones, and strikers Maurice Tadman and Wilf Carter. This squad, if assembled now, would surely grace the Premiership!'

TORQUAY 0 EXETER 2
Fourth Division, 14 April 1990
(Attendance 3,389)

United (5-3-2): Ken Veysey; Peter Whiston, Phil Lloyd, Al Hannigan (sub: Matt Elliot), John Uzzell, Paul Holmes; Mark Loram, Sean Joyce, John Morrison; Dave Caldwell (sub: Steve Cookson), Dean Edwards; Manager: Dave Smith. City (4-4-2): Kevin Miller; Scott Hiley, Jim McNichol, Shaun Taylor, Angus McPherson; Brian McDermott, Danny Bailey, Tom Kelly, Richard Dryden; Richard Young, Steve Neville; Manager: Terry Cooper.

Top of the table Exeter City eased their way to victory and completed the double over their derby rivals. The visitors were promotion favourites, despite a poor away record, but they did not need to be at their best to inflict United's third successive home defeat. A spirited Torquay side kept the result in doubt until the final whistle, but in truth they never looked capable of blocking City's triumphant surge to the championship of the Fourth Division.

On a bitterly cold and blustery day at Plainmoor, the crowd had little to cheer about in a featureless first half. Playing with the wind at their backs, the Gulls created the best chance after eleven minutes when Dean Edwards set up Dave Caldwell with a low cross from the right. The striker missed a golden opportunity by blazing his first-time shot wide of the target from eight yards. The gifted but temperamental Caldwell was United's most threatening forward in more

Jim McNichol fires in a shot against Torquay.

ways than one. After he had kicked out at Danny Bailey and been booked for a foul on Shaun Taylor, manager Dave Smith substituted him at half-time to prevent a further blot appearing on one of the worst disciplinary records in soccer.

The all-important opening goal came after sixty-three minutes, when former United player Tom Kelly swung in a beautifully curving free-kick from the right to pick out unmarked skipper Shaun Taylor, who thundered a header past 'keeper Ken Veysey. Future Leicester and Scotland star, Matt Elliott, almost levelled the scores ten minutes from time. The substitute beat 'keeper Kevin Miller with a superb header from a Mark Loram free-kick, but full-back Scott Hiley had positioned himself perfectly to clear the ball off the line. City repelled the home side's last ditch attacks, then broke out to snatch a second goal in injury time. Left-back Angus McPherson, on loan from Glasgow Rangers, collected the ball on the halfway line and evaded a series of challenges before nonchalantly chipping the ball over Veysey and into the roof of the net from 20 yards. Despite losing 13 away games, Terry Cooper's team went on to win the title by a margin of ten points. It was the only time in their history that Exeter had been promoted as champions. Torquay took the hard route to match their neighbours' achievement a year later, when they won promotion in a play-off final against Blackpool at Wembley Stadium. The Gulls' triumph was short-lived, however, as they were immediately relegated back down to the basement League after only one season in the rarefied atmosphere of the Third Division.

EXETER CITY 2 PLYMOUTH 3
Division Two, 2 March 1994
(Attendance 6,601)

City (4-4-2): Peter Fox; Jason Minett, Scott Daniels, Robbie Turner, Ron Robinson; Stuart Storer, Mark Cooper, Russell Coughlin, Mark Gavin; Mickey Ross (sub: Jon Brown), Nicky Morgan (sub: David Adekola); Manager: Terry Cooper.
Argyle (4-3-3): Alan Nicholls; Mark Patterson, Keith Hill (sub: Alan McCarthy), Andy Comyn, Dominic Naylor; Steve McCall, Wayne Burnett, Steve Castle; Craig Skinner, Kevin Nugent, Mickey Evans; Manager: Peter Shilton.

Former England goalkeeper Peter Shilton celebrated his second anniversary as manager of Plymouth Argyle by laying the St James Park hoodoo. In a pulsating derby, which was the forty-fifth League meeting of the old rivals, the Pilgrims climbed to second place in the table by winning their first League match at the ground since 1928, and simultaneously plunged the Grecians into deep relegation trouble.

During the first half, underdogs Exeter looked capable of upsetting the form book and maintaining their proud sixty-six-year home record against a tentative Plymouth team. The better football came from the home side, and they gave the Argyle defence an early scare when Nicky Morgan out-jumped marker Andy Comyn to head a Mark Gavin cross against the crossbar. Following a period of sustained pressure, City deservedly took the lead on the half-hour. Jason Minett's volley was deflected by Keith Hill into the path of Mark Cooper. The midfielder let fly and tucked away a low shot past 'keeper Alan Nichols, who had just been selected for the England Under 21 squad.

Argyle came out fighting in the second half and transformed the match by snatching two quick goals to overtake City within seven minutes of the restart. They

Mark Cooper opened the scoring for City.

levelled when Mark Patterson charged into the box and, as 'keeper Peter Fox rushed out to block him, the full-back hit a low cross which covering defender Mark Gavin unluckily deflected into his own net. The home side were then left reeling when Mickey Evans broke free on the left and cut the ball back perfectly for Wayne Burnett to side-foot Argyle into the lead. In a vain attempt to turn the tide, City boss Terry Cooper brought on Jon Brown for Mickey Ross and pushed former Pilgrim Robbie Turner forward. This did not prevent a rampant Argyle side from increasing their lead in the seventy-sixth minute with the best goal of the game. From a throw-in on the right, Kevin Nugent turned his marker and the striker's low cross to the near post was hammered into the roof of the net from close range by Mickey Evans. Exeter substitute David Adekola replaced Nicky Morgan and pulled one back when Turner and Cooper combined to lay the ball off to the Nigerian international, who drove past Alan Nichols.

The Grecians were doomed to relegation and the Pilgrims subsequently lost impetus and missed out on automatic promotion, before losing a two-leg play-off tie against Burnley. A year later, dreams of Division One soccer seemed a distant memory in the fluctuating fortunes of soccer, as Argyle were at the opposite end of the table heading to join neighbours City in Division Three.

The 'Sunday Independent' published Mike Holgate's choice for Exeter City's greatest players in their 'Millennium Moments in Sport' edition:

'Dick Pym, who never conceded a goal in three FA Cup final appearances at Wembley for Bolton Wanderers in the 1920s, is the natural choice for custodian of my great Grecians. Pre-war crowd favourite Charlie Miller occupies the left-back berth, while on the opposite flank is Theo Foley, who later played for Northampton during their rise from the Third Division to the top flight during the 1960s. Inter-war stalwart Jack Angus is at the heart of the defence alongside popular Jimmy Giles – voted Exeter's player of the year for two consecutive seasons in 1971/72 and 1972/73. 1920s kingpin Ellis Crompton patrols the midfield with Maurice Setters, who left City for West Bromwich Albion, and later won an FA Cup winners medal with Manchester United in 1963. Exeter-born winger Cliff Bastin became one of England's greatest players, after joining Arsenal in 1929, and has rightfully been inducted into soccer's Hall of Fame. Striker Tony Kellow – recently voted City's greatest player by the club's fans - would form a potent strike force with Eire international Dermot Curtis and hard-shooting Harold Blackmore, who scored in Bolton's 1929 FA Cup final win. Sitting it out on the bench, waiting for their chance to shine would be three pre-war players: goalkeeper Arthur Davies, stalwart defender Stan Charlton, midfielder Harold 'Happy' Houghton, with two post-war natural goalscorers, Fred Binney and Alan Banks.'

EXETER CITY 1 PLYMOUTH ARGYLE 1
Division Three, 23 March 1996
(Attendance 6,195)

City (4-3-3): Peter Fox (player-manager); Neil Parsley, Noel Blake, Mark Came, Darren Hughes; Danny Bailey, Jon Richardson, Mark Cooper; Mark Gavin, Leon Braithwaite, Adrian Foster (sub: John Sharpe 59 mins – sub: Colin Anderson 87 mins).
Argyle (4-4-2): Steve Cherry; Mark Patterson, Richard Logan, Mick Heathcote, Paul Williams; Chris Billy, Gary Clayton, Ian Baird, Martin Barlow; Adrian Littlejohn, Mickey Evans; Manager: Neil Warnock.

On the eve of this derby, Plymouth Argyle defenders Mick Heathcote and Paul Williams received recognition from their fellow professionals when they were named in the Professional Footballers Association Division Three Team of the Year. However, in a one-sided contest at St James Park, an outclassed City side showed that they also had useful defenders with brilliant performances from 'keeper Peter Fox and central defenders Noel Blake and Mark Came, which held the promotion-hopefuls to a draw.

On New Year's Day, the City underdogs had come away from Home Park leaving Argyle grateful for a point, and the return also ended in a frustrating stalemate for the visitors. Plymouth were at full strength against an injury-plagued City side, with debut boy Adrian Foster meeting his team-mates for the first time in the dressing room before the kick-off. The Argyle attack immediately clicked quickly into gear and earned a ninth-minute lead with a superb strike from Gary Clayton. After good work by Chris Billy and Ian Baird, the veteran midfielder hit a 25-yard swerving drive between two defenders, who were attempting to close him down, and the ball flew past an unsighted Peter Fox. Ten minutes later, City finally broke out of defence and winger Mark Gavin swung a long ball to the far post, which defender Mark Patterson failed to clear. The ball was hit back into the box by Mark Cooper, and Richard Logan instinctively stuck out a foot and deflected it into his own net. This fluke enabled the Grecians to mount a second-half backs-to-the-wall effort, as Argyle's midfield quartet of Chris Billy, Gary Clayton, Ian Baird and Martin Barlow ploughed through the clinging mud, running City into the ground. Strikers Adrian Littlejohn and Mickey Evans were a constant menace, but even if they got the better of central defenders Noel Blake and Mark Came, they were denied by the flying brilliance of Peter Fox. The Grecians almost snatched an unlikely winner when the redoubtable Mark Came temporarily abandoned his defensive duties and moved up to head a Mark Gavin cross inches over the bar.

Despite this derby setback, Argyle finished fourth in the table and, after defeating Colchester in a two-leg promotion play-off, set up their first appearance at Wembley – where a Ronnie Mauge goal against Darlington was enough to book their passage into Division Two. Manager Neil Warnock's team-building plans were blocked by the board and he departed, leaving his assistant Mick Jones to steer the club away from relegation trouble before the club dropped the following season and were re-united with Exeter and Torquay in the basement League.

Argyle scorer Gary Clayton tangles with City's Leon Braithwaite.

The 'Sunday Independent' revealed Mike Holgate's choice of Torquay United's greatest players in the 'Millennium Moments in Sport' edition:

'Ignoring the claims of many great players, including Bruce Rioch and Neville Southall, who came to Torquay towards the end of their careers – my side contains six internationals who were developed by the club. Three of these are still playing – Lee Sharpe (now with Bradford, formerly of Manchester United and England), Matt Elliot (Leicester and Scotland), and Rodney Jack (Crewe and St Vincent). 1960s midfield battler Jimmy Dunne was capped by Eire after moving to Fulham. Centre half Don Welsh captained Charlton in the first two post-war FA Cup finals at inside forward, and also won England caps at wing-half. Winger Ralph Birkett starred for Arsenal and then Middlesborough, where he was called up by England in 1936, temporarily displacing the great Stanley Matthews. The Gulls have been served by many fine goalkeepers, but Mike Mahoney gets my vote after proving himself in the top flight with Newcastle in the 1970s. Full-back Syd Cann also went on to play at the highest level with Manchester City in the 1933 FA Cup final, and was a member of the Charlton Athletic side which finished runners-up in the old First Division in 1937. 1950s midfield maestro Don Mills is an automatic choice, having been recently voted the club's greatest-ever player by United fans. Completing the side are the club's two most prolific strikers – Sammy Collins, who scored a club record 42 goals during the 1955/56 season, and 1960s golden boy Robin Stubbs. Post-war players on the subs bench are goalkeeper Terry Adlington, free-scoring winger Ron Shaw, midfield schemer Tommy Mitchinson, versatile defender Alan Smith, and play-anywhere Clint Boulton.'

TORQUAY UNITED 2 EXETER CITY 1
Division Three, 20 January 2001
(Attendance 4,055)

United (4-4-2): Ryan Northmore; Steve Tully, Jimmy Aggrey, Lee Russell, Robbie Herrera (sub: Paul Holmes); Khalid Chalqui, Gary Neil, Mark Ford, Kevin Hill (sub: Kevin Parker); Eifion Williams, Tony Bedeau (sub: John Gayle); Manager: Wes Saunders.
City (4-4-2): Arjan Van Heusden; Neil Whitworth, Chris Curran, Noel Blake (player-manager – sub: Mark Burrows), Graeme Power; Christian Roberts (sub: Graeme Tomlinson), Paul Buckle; John Cornworth (sub: Kwame Ampadu), Mark Rawlinson, Paul Read, Steve Flack.

'Probably the most critical Devon derby of all time' was how one tabloid sports journalist described this match between two sides in the bottom three hovering above Carlisle who had four games in hand. Dire recent form indicated that a win for either side could condemn their rivals to the brink of non-League oblivion!

The match got off to a sensational start when City skipper Chris Curran was red-carded after five minutes for elbowing Khalid Chalqi. In fact, the visitors

Gulls skipper Mark Ford strokes home the first goal of the match from the spot.

seemed hell-bent on beating their record of ten bookings in a match – accumulated a month earlier – as four of their players were shown the yellow card in the first half. The crude defensive tactics of the depleted Grecians contained United until the stroke of half time, when a rash challenge by John Cornworth brought down striker Tony Bedeau from behind. The referee had no hesitation in pointing to the spot and pandemonium broke out as home skipper Mark Ford put his side in front and sparked a pitch invasion with an over-the-top victory jig in front of the Exeter fans.

A disciplined approach after the interval transformed City with forward Christian Roberts showing impressive close skills which tormented the home side, and it was no more than the visitors deserved when he set up the chance for Mark Rawlinson to blast home an equaliser in the seventieth minute. Exeter squandered good chances to clinch the match but just as the teams seemed ready to settle for a point apiece, the game was decided by a Plymouthian – substitute Kevin Parker – who was introduced by the Gulls in the eighty-ninth minute. Deep into injury time, he darted through the City defence and chipped the ball over the sprawling 'keeper, and was then promptly booked for removing his shirt in celebration.

'Someone at this club must have run over a black cat and reversed back over it to finish the job,' groaned John Cornworth to waiting newsmen, as this result piled on the agony for the Grecians. However, watching the game was Spurs legend Steve Perryman. He agreed to assist player-manager Noel Blake as an unpaid 'football consultant' and the club's fortunes improved enough to ease them clear of the relegation mire. As the season drew to a nerve-tingling climax, it was Torquay who were facing League extinction. Plymouth Argyle publicly wished the Gulls well and Exeter City sportingly sent the club a good luck fax signed by all the players, as fate decreed that United's survival depended on coming away from Barnet with at least a point in an end-of-season cliff-hanger which resulted in yet another 'Great Escape'. A 3-2 victory thrilled the hordes of travelling supporters and condemned their North London opponents to the 'Big Drop'!

STATISTICS
Football League Derby Results 1920-2001
(home team score on left-hand side of each column)

| Season | Plymouth *v.* Exeter | | Exeter *v.* Torquay | | Torquay *v.* Plymouth | |
	Argyle	City	City	United	United	Argyle
1920/21	0-0	1-1	-	-	-	-
1921/22	0-0	0-2	-	-	-	-
1922/23	5-1	0-0	-	-	-	-
1923/24	4-0	0-4	-	-	-	-
1924/25	1-1	3-0	-	-	-	-
1925/26	2-2	4-0	-	-	-	-
1926/27	2-0	0-2	-	-	-	-
1927/28	1-2	2-0	5-0	1-1	1-2	4-1
1928/29	0-0	1-2	1-3	1-3	2-2	4-0
1929/30	4-1	1-1	0-0	2-1	3-4	5-0
1930/31	-	-	2-2	0-0	-	-
1931/32	-	-	3-1	2-1	-	-
1932/33	-	-	5-0	1-3	-	-
1933/34	-	-	4-0	0-2	-	-
1934/35	-	-	1-1	3-0	-	-
1935/36	-	-	1-1	2-1	-	-
1936/37	-	-	2-1	0-1	-	-
1937/38	-	-	2-0	2-1	-	-
1938/39	-	-	1-2	0-1	-	-
1946/47	-	-	1-1	2-1	-	-

The Torquay United squad which won promotion from the Fourth Division in 1960.

Jubilant Gulls celebrate their 1991 play-off victory at Wembley.

Season	Plymouth v. Exeter		Exeter v. Torquay		Torquay v. Plymouth	
	Argyle	City	City	United	United	Argyle
1947/48	-	-	0-2	1-2	-	-
1948/49	-	-	2-0	2-1	-	-
1949/50	-	-	1-1	1-4	-	-
1950/51	0-1	3-2	0-0	2-0	1-3	1-0
1951/52	2-1	1-0	4-0	5-1	3-2	2-2
1952/53	-	-	4-1	5-2	-	-
1953/54	-	-	1-2	3-2	-	-
1954/55	-	-	1-2	1-0	-	-
1955/56	-	-	0-0	3-1	-	-
1956/57	5-0	2-1	1-1	1-0	1-1	0-0
1957/58	1-0	4-2	5-1	1-3	0-2	1-0
1958/59	-	-	2-2	3-4	-	-
1959/60	-	-	1-0	2-3	-	-
1960/61	-	-	-	-	-	-
1961/62	-	-	-	-	-	-
1962/63	-	-	0-3	3-0	-	-
1963/64	-	-	0-0	1-1	-	-
1964/65	-	-	-	-	-	-
1965/66	-	-	-	-	-	-
1966/67	-	-	-	-	-	-
1967/68	-	-	-	-	-	-
1968/69	-	-	-	-	0-1	1-0
1969/70	-	-	-	-	1-2	6-0
1970/71	-	-	-	-	2-1	1-2
1971/72	-	-	-	-	2-1	3-1
1972/73	-	-	3-2	0-2	-	-
1973/74	-	-	4-2	0-0	-	-
1974/75	-	-	0-0	2-2	-	-
1975/76	-	-	0-0	1-0	-	-
1976/77	-	-	3-0	0-1	-	-
1977/78	2-2	0-0	-	-	-	-
1978/79	4-2	1-0	-	-	-	-
1979/80	2-0	2-2	-	-	-	-
1980/81	0-2	1-1	-	-	-	-
1981/82	2-1	1-1	-	-	-	-

Plymouth Argyle – champions of the Third Division in 1930.

| Season | Plymouth v. Exeter | | Exeter v. Torquay | | Torquay v. Plymouth | |
	Argyle	City	City	United	United	Argyle
1982/83	1-0	1-0	-	-	-	-
1983/84	2-2	1-1	-	-	-	-
1984/85	-	-	4-3	1-1	-	-
1985/86	-	-	2-2	1-2	-	-
1986/87	-	-	2-2	1-1	-	-
1987/88	-	-	0-1	1-1	-	-
1988/89	-	-	3-0	0-4	-	-
1989/90	-	-	3-0	0-2	-	-
1990/91	-	-	-	-	-	-
1991/92	-	-	1-0	1-0	-	-
1992/93	0-3	2-0	-	-	-	-
1993/94	1-0	2-3	-	-	-	-
1994/95	-	-	1-2	0-0	-	-
1995/96	2-2	1-1	0-0	0-2	0-2	4-3
1996/97	-	-	1-1	2-0	-	-
1997/98	-	-	1-1	1-2	-	-
1998/99	1-0	1-1	1-1	1-0	1-1	0-0
1999/2000	1-0	1-1	3-2	1-0	0-4	2-2
2000/01	1-0	0-2	1-1	2-1	1-0	3-1

Summary

| Plymouth v. Exeter | | | | Exeter v. Torquay | | | | Torquay v. Plymouth | | | |
Argyle		City		City		United		United		Argyle	
P	W	W	D	P	W	W	D	P	W	W	D
54	21	14	19	94	36	29	29	30	5	19	8

Devon Football League Records 1920/21-2000/01

Season	Plymouth	Exeter	Torquay	Summary of Ups and Downs
1920/21	11th D3	19th D3	-	*Founding of the Third Division
1921/22	2nd D3S	21st D3S	-	*The first of six seasons when Argyle
1922/23	2nd D3S	20th D3S	-	finished as runners-up when only
1923/24	2nd D3S	16th D3S	-	champs promoted
1924/25	2nd D3S	7th D3S	-	
1925/26	2nd D3S	20th D3S	-	
1926/27	2nd D3S	12th D3S	1st SL	*Torquay elected to FL
1927/28	3rd D3S	8th D3S	22nd D3S	*United re-elected to FL
1928/29	4th D3S	21st D3S	18th D3S	
1929/30	1st D3S	16th D3S	19th D3S	*Argyle promoted to D2
1930/31	18th D2	13th D3S	11th D3S	
1931/32	4th D2	7th D3S	19th D3S	
1932/33	14th D2	2nd D3S	10th D3S	* Runners-up City miss out
1933/34	10th D2	9th D3S	20th D3S	
1934/35	8th D2	11th D3S	10th D3S	
1935/36	7th D2	22th D3S	10th D3S	* City re-elected to FL
1936/37	5th D2	21st D3S	20th D3S	
1937/38	13th D2	17th D3S	20th D3S	
1938/39	15th D2	14th D3S	19th D3S	
1939/40	League programme abandoned due to outbreak of the Second World War			
1946/47	19th D2	15th D3S	11th D3S	
1947/48	17th D2	11th D3S	18th D3S	
1948/49	20th D2	12th D3S	9th D3S	
1949/50	21st D2	16th D3S	5th D3S	*Argyle relegated to D3S
1950/51	4th D3S	14th D3S	20th D3S	
1951/52	1st D3S	23th D3S	11th D3S	
1952/53	4th D2	17th D3S	12th D3S	*Argyle promoted to D2
1953/54	19th D2	9th D3S	13th D3S	
1954/55	20th D2	22th D3S	8th D3S	

Exeter City celebrate their promotion to the Third Division in 1964.

Season	Plymouth	Exeter	Torquay	Summary of Ups and Downs
1955/56	21st D2	16th D3S	5th D3S	*Argyle relegated to D3S
1956/57	18th D3S	21st D3S	2nd D3S	*Torquay miss out on goal average
1957/58	3th D3S	24th D3S	21st D3S	

Regional Divisions 3 (North) and (South) are scrapped – United and City's lowly finish mean that they drop to the newly created Division Four

Season	Plymouth	Exeter	Torquay	Summary of Ups and Downs
1958/59	1st D3	5th D4	12th D4	*Argyle promoted to D2
1959/60	19th D2	9th D4	3rd D4	*United promoted to D3
1960/61	11th D2	21st D4	12th D3	
1961/62	5th D2	18th D4	21st D3	*United relegated to D4
1962/63	12th D2	17th D4	6th D4	
1963/64	20th D2	4th D4	6th D4	*City promoted to D3
1964/65	15th D2	17th D3	11th D4	
1965/66	18th D2	22nd D3	3rd D4	*United promoted to D3/City relegated to D4
1966/67	16th D2	14th D4	7th D3	
1967/68	22th D2	20th D4	4th D3	*Argyle drop to D3
1968/69	5th D3	17th D4	6th D3	
1969/70	17th D3	18th D4	13th D3	
1970/71	15th D3	9th D4	10th D3	
1971/72	8th D3	15th D4	23rd D3	*United drop to D4
1972/73	8th D3	8th D4	18th D4	
1973/74	17th D3	10th D4	16th D4	
1974/75	2nd D3	9th D4	14th D4	Argyle promoted to D2
1975/76	16th D2	7th D4	9th D4	
1976/77	21st D2	2nd D4	16th D4	Argyle and City take different routes to D3
1977/78	19th D3	17th D3	9th D4	
1978/79	15th D3	9th D3	11th D4	
1979/80	15th D3	8th D3	9th D4	
1980/81	7th D3	11th D3	17th D4	
1981/82	10th D3	18th D3	15th D4	
1982/83	8th D3	19th D3	12th D4	
1983/84	19th D3	24th D3	9th D4	*City relegated to D4
1984/85	15th D3	19th D4	24th D4	*United re-elected to FL
1985/86	2nd D3	21st D4	24th D4	*Argyle promoted to D2/TQ and EX re-elected

League is re-structured to allow annual entry of non-league club at expense of bottom club in Football League. United narrowly avoid this fate by gaining a point in the last match of the season

Season	Plymouth	Exeter	Torquay	Summary of Ups and Downs
1986/87	7th D2	14th D4	23rd D4	
1987/88	16th D2	22nd D4	5th D4	
1888/89	18th D2	13th D4	14th D4	
1989/90	16th D2	1st D4	15th D4	*City promoted to D4
1990/91	18th D2	16th D3	7th D4	*TQ promoted to Wembley play-off final
1991/92	22nd D2	20th D3	23rd D3	*United re-elected to FL

Premier League is introduced and Divisions 1, 2, 3 replace 2, 3, 4

Season	Plymouth	Exeter	Torquay	Summary of Ups and Downs
1992/93	14th D2	19th D2	19th D3	
1993/94	3rd D2	22nd D2	6th D3	
1994/95	21st D2	22nd D3	13th D3	*Argyle relegated to D3/Only the ineligibility of Conference champs Macclesfield Town's ground saves City from non-league oblivion
1995/96	4th D3	14th D3	24th D3	* Argyle win Wembley play-off final. United avoid the 'big drop' when ground regulations prevent the Conference champions Stevenage from taking their place
1996/97	19th D2	22nd D3	21st D3	
1997/98	22nd D2	15th D3	5th D3	*United lose play-off final at Wembley. Argyle drop down to join them and Exeter in D3
1998/99	13th D3	12th D3	20th D3	
1999/2000	12th D3	9th D3	21st D3	
2000/01	13th D3	19th D3	21st D3	*United win last match of season at Barnet to pull off another 'Great Escape'

2

HAT-TRICK HEROES

Argyle's Paul McGregor holds aloft the match ball, after scoring a hat-trick at Torquay in March 2000. In 178 League derbies between Devon clubs, this feat has been achieved on only twelve occasions!

PLYMOUTH ARGYLE 5 EXETER CITY 1
THIRD DIVISION (SOUTH), 30 MARCH 1923
(ATTENDANCE 16,000)

Argyle (2-3-5): Fred Craig; Billy Forbes, Moses Russell; Jimmy Logan, Jack Hill, Alf Rowe; Patsy Corcoran, Rollo Jack, Jack Fowler, Bert Batten, Billy Baker; Manager: Robert Jack.
City (2-3-5): Syd Pavey; Bob Pollard, John Ackroyd; Len Southway, Jim Mitton, Ellis Crompton; Alf Matthews, John Davis, Harry Crockford, Allan Mathieson, John Dockray; Manager: Fred Mavin.

During the 1920s, Plymouth Argyle were blessed with a succession of prolific strikers whose goals brought them close to promotion on several occasions before it was eventually achieved in 1930. The roll of honour of leading marksmen included Jack Cock, Ray Bowden, Frank Richardson, Percy Richards, Percy Cherrett, Fred Forbes and Jack Fowler, who became the first man to score a hat-trick in a Devon League derby!

When Exeter City took an early lead, they could not have envisaged conceding five goals and leaving Home Park well beaten by a brilliant display of

JACK FOWLER.
SWANSEA TOWN.

JOHN FOWLER

Jack Fowler won international honours with Swansea.

opportunism from Jack Fowler. Straight from the kick-off, the visitors attacked strongly and, after five minutes, Alf Matthews beat Moses Russell on the right and passed to fellow winger John Dockray, whose snap-shot was handled by full-back Billy Forbes. Harry Crockford slotted his spot-kick effortlessly past 'keeper Fred Craig to put the Grecians one up. Argyle hit back immediately, and City had a lucky escape when Jack Fowler slipped the ball through to Bert Batten. The inside forward badly mishit an attempted shot, which spun to the feet of left-winger Billy Baker, whose first-time drive cannoned off the post. The Pilgrims deservedly pulled level in the twenty-fifth minute, when winger Patsy Corcoran waltzed round defenders Ellis Crompton and Harry Ackroyd to create a chance for his inside partner, Rollo Jack, which was converted from close range.

Argyle took the lead five minutes after the interval, when Fowler made the most of an opening created by Billy Baker. Patsy Corcoran then wove more magic on the right wing, and his shot was defected onto the upright by City centre half Jim Mitton, and Fowler snapped up the rebound to put the home side two in front. The centre forward completed his hat-trick by out-jumping the defence to head a Baker corner past helpless 'keeper Syd Pavey. Patsy Corcoran wrapped up the scoring by eluding Crompton to beat Pavey with the best shot of the match.

Jack Fowler collected 17 goals in 22 League games, as Plymouth missed promotion by finishing divisional runners-up in 1922/23. Despite his obvious goal-scoring talent, he was never an automatic choice for the first team during his time at Home Park. After scoring a further 7 goals in only 10 appearances the following season, Swansea paid a then club record fee of £1,280 in March 1924 to take the striker back to his native country. The Swans' faith was fully justified, as Jack hit 100 goals in seven seasons – including nine hat-tricks, a five and a four. He was also honoured by Wales and capped 6 times. Argyle were made to regret their decision to sell when the centre forward's goals took Swansea to the championship of Third Division (South) in 1924/25, leaving the Pilgrims floundering once again in second spot.

PLYMOUTH ARGYLE 4 TORQUAY UNITED 1
DIVISION THREE (SOUTH), 17 MARCH 1928
(ATTENDANCE 9,008)

Argyle (2-3-5): George Stanbury; Moses Russell, Walter Price; Fred McKenzie, John Pullen, Alec Hardie; Alf Matthews, Norman Mackay, Percy Richards, Jack Leslie, Sammy Black; Manager: Robert Jack.
United (2-3-5): Archie Bayes; Maurice Wellock, Jack Price; Claude Gough, Hugh Good, Frank Wragge; Jim Mackey, Tom McGovern, Bert Turner, Alwyn Thomas, Jack Pattison; Manager: Percy Mackrill.

The carnival atmosphere which enveloped Plainmoor at the start of their first campaign in the Football League soon dissipated, after a bright start when they drew at home with Exeter on the opening day of the season. By the time the Magpies arrived to make their first appearance as a League club at Home Park, the party was well and truly over, as they were firmly entrenched at the bottom of the League and heading for re-election. Plymouth were facing a different crisis, as they had lost their two previous home games and were anxious to put their promotion bid back on track. Making only his 10th appearance for Argyle, was centre forward Percy Richards. Signed from Burnley in the New Year, he had scored five goals, including two on his debut, and was about to go one better in his first appearance

Alf Matthews – the best goal of the match!

in a Devon derby.

Argyle skipper Moses Russell won the toss and gained a material advantage by leaving his opponents facing a strong wind. All the home side's goals came in the first half, and Percy Richards collected his hat-trick in a stunning ten-minute spell midway through the session. He scored the opener after twenty-five minutes, in a well-worked move with right-winger Alf Matthews, who swung over a pinpoint centre, which provided a simple tap-in chance. Inside right Norman Mackay and left-winger Sammy Black supplied further openings, both of which Richards clinically converted to put the Pilgrims three up. During a period of sustained pressure, Percy came close to adding to his tally, but was denied by the brilliance of former England amateur international goalkeeper Archie Bayes, who made two fantastic saves from point-blank range. However, this Argyle performance was no one-man show, and the finest goal of the match came from Alf Matthews, just before the interval. He had tormented United throughout the half, and rounded off a fine display with a well-deserved goal. A solo run through a bewildered defence ended with a glorious cross shot which gave Bayes no chance.

Torquay carried the attack to their opponents in the second half, in a belated effort to salvage some pride. Within two minutes of the restart they had reduced the arrears, when leading scorer Bert Turner beat John Pullen and lobbed the ball over advancing 'keeper Gordon Stanbury. The ball bounced back off the crossbar and was scrambled away by Pullen only as far as left-winger Pattison, whose fierce shot caused Moses Russell to head into his own net. Argyle could not be accused of sitting back on their lead, and only desperate defending kept the United attack at bay. Several shots narrowly missed the target, but despite dominating play for the rest of the game, Torquay could not close the gap.

Plymouth won their 5 remaining home games that season and Percy Richards notched 10 goals in 18 appearances. Despite this late surge, they could only finish in third place, breaking their incredible sequence of six seasons as divisional runners-up.

Devon's top League scorers between the wars were Jack Cock (Argyle, 33 goals, 1927); Fred Whitlow (City, 33 goals, 1933) and Jimmy Trotter (United, 26 goals, 1931). The postwar records are held by Tommy Tynan (Argyle, 31 goals, 1985); Fred Binney (City, 28 goals, 1973); and Sam Collins (United, 40 goals, 1956). Seven strikers have topped the goalscoring charts of two Devon clubs (year in brackets show when first achieved for each club): Cyril Hemingway (Torquay 1929, Exeter 1930); Ernie Edds (Plymouth 1948, Torquay 1952); Mike Trebilcock (Plymouth 1965, Torquay 1973); Alan Welsh (Torquay 1972, Plymouth 1973); Fred Binney (Exeter 1972, Plymouth 1979); John Sims (Plymouth 1982, Torquay 1984); and Dean Edwards (Exeter 1988, Torquay 1989).

PLYMOUTH ARGYLE 4 TORQUAY UNITED 0
THIRD DIVISION (SOUTH), 29 MARCH 1929
(ATTENDANCE 15,000)

Argyle (2-3-5): Fred Craig; Harry Bland, Moses Russell; Norman Mackay, Fred Mackenzie, John Pullen; Alf Matthews, Frank Sloan, Percy Richards, Jack Leslie, Sammy Black; Manager; Robert Jack.
United (2-3-5): Harold Gough; Jim Mellon, Billy Brown; Arthur Smeaton, Jim Carrick, Bob Smith; Dan Kelly, Joe Hill, Wally Gardner, Cyril Hemmingway, Harry Waller; Manager: Percy Mackrill.

During his second season at Plymouth, Percy Richards found his first team appearances restricted by the emergence of future England international Ray Bowden. However, he made the most of only his sixth League outing of the season in this Easter Derby.

His second hat-trick in two games against United gave Argyle their first win in nine games. For Torquay, again struggling near the foot of the division, this was to be the fourth game in a row when they failed to find the net. The Good Friday crowd at Home Park saw a niggling opening to the match. Tempers began to fray, as players on both sides were guilty of over-zealous tackles. The referee spoke to several culprits before the first half ended in stalemate.

Percy Richards had claimed a first-half hat-trick in his first outing against Torquay, and if the United defenders thought they had quelled the threat as they walked off to the dressing-room at the interval, they were in for a nasty shock. The Pilgrims took the lead early in the second period, when Richards rose to head an Alf Matthews free-kick awarded just outside the area. The second came following a blunder by full-back Billy Brown, which set Percy off on a solo run ending with a fierce shot struck past former England 'keeper Harold Gough. A chance for Plymouth's third arrived when Bob Smith handled in the penalty area, but John Pullen was nominated to take the spot-kick and dragged his shot wide of the upright.

The penalty miss proved to be a temporary reprieve for the Magpies, as the result was put beyond doubt following a Matthews corner. Sammy Black miscued his shot, but the ball fell at the feet of Norman Mackay, who tapped it calmly into the net. The best goal was saved until last, as Percy Richards collected his third, and his team's fourth of the match. Alf Matthews swung over a cross which Percy met on the half-volley, hitting a thunderbolt through a crowded penalty area.

Argyle completed the double over United in the return game at Plainmoor on Easter Monday. On this occasion, Percy Richards did not find the net as he was carried off injured following a collision with the goalkeeper. Yet, how he must have wished he could face Torquay United every week! His goal-scoring feats against the Magpies did not secure a place in the Argyle side. In fact, he made only one first-team appearance during the club's successful promotion

Percy Richards (kneeling, second from left) pictured during his playing days at Burnley.

campaign the following season. Leaving Plymouth in 1931, Percy ended his playing days with non-League clubs, Tunbridge Wells and Folkstone. His record is unique as, seventy years on, he remains the only player to have collected more than one League hat-trick in Devon derbies.

At the end of the twentieth century, soccer magazine 'Total Football' conducted a survey to discover which goal qualified as the greatest-ever for each club. Top of the polls for Plymouth was Ronnie Mauge's headed winner against Darlington in the 1996 promotion play-off final at Wembley. There was also strong support for Andy Roger's direct in-swinging corner at Derby in 1994 and Fred Binney's relegation-saving effort against Port Vale in 1978. Reliving that Wembley moment was supporter Matt Hunkin: 'I waited for what seemed like an age for the back of the net, in those deep Wembley goals, to halt the flight of the ball'.

PLYMOUTH ARGYLE 4 EXETER CITY 1
THIRD DIVISION (SOUTH), 26 OCTOBER 1929
(ATTENDANCE 15,427)

Argyle (2-3-5): Fred Craig; Harry Bland, Freddie Titmuss; Norman Mackay, John Pullen, Alec Hardie; Tommy Grozier, Frank Sloan, Ray Bowden, Jack Leslie, Sammy Black; Manager: Bob Jack.
City (2-3-5): John Alderson; George Howson, Charlie Miller; Reg Clarke, Jock Ditchburn, Dave McMullan; George Purcell, Harry Houghton, George Guyan, Cyril Hemingway, Arthur Doncaster; Manager; Billy McDevitt.

Cornishman Ray Bowden had been discovered playing for Looe, and displayed the class which was to gain him international honours, with 21 goals in 29 games during his first full League campaign. Established as leader of the attack, he started the following season in prime form and, after this match, he had improved his goal ratio to one a game, with 9 goals from 9 League outings.

The writing was on the wall for Exeter after four minutes, when Ray Bowden finished off a glorious Argyle move. Midfield general Jack Leslie found Bowden with a telling pass, the ball was pushed out to wing-wizard Sammy Black, whose centre was half-cleared to Norman McKay. The half-back sent Tommy Grozier away down the right and the winger's accurate cross was met by Bowden, who made no mistake from close range. The Pilgrims were so much in control of the match that it came as a total surprise when the visitors levelled against the run of play after nineteen minutes. Cyril Hemmingway skilfully controlled a high ball and completed a fine solo run by firing past 'keeper Fred Craig. All Exeter's good work was undone two minutes later when the home side were gifted a soft goal. Ray Bowden stubbed his toe as he struck a shot which somehow trickled into the net through the grasp of horrified 'keeper John Alderson. Sammy Black completed the Grecians' first half misery by scoring the best goal of the match just before half time. He cut inside to meet a ball from Grozier and hit a ferocious volley which flew into the net.

Plymouth appeared to ease off after the interval and the Grecians worked hard to reduce the arrears without luck. The home side were somewhat fortunate to increase their lead against the run of play, when Ray Bowden completed his first League hat-trick. Argyle broke quickly out of defence, and Tommy Grozier dribbled half the length of the field, before striking a stunning shot which was brilliantly palmed away by the 'keeper, only to leave a simple tap-in chance for the lurking striker. Ray Bowden might have added to his impressive haul, but missed the easiest chance of the match just before the final whistle.

In 1931, Ray was chosen to represent an FA team on a tour of Canada, and his goal-scoring feats began to attract the attention of the big clubs. In March 1933, Arsenal paid a £5,000 club record fee for his services. Ray appeared in the same forward line as Exeter's Cliff Bastin and Torquay's Ralph Birkett for the

*Ray Bowden won top honours with the
Gunners.*

Gunners, who had established themselves as the world's most famous club
under manager Herbert Chapman. At Highbury, Ray was in the side which won
the League championship in 1935 and the FA Cup in 1936. He was also awarded
6 England caps, before moving to Newcastle United. When his playing days
were over, he became a familiar sight back in Plymouth, behind the counter of
his own sports shop.

*Exeter supporters' choice for most memorable goal of the twentieth
century, in a survey conducted by 'Total Football', was Martin Phillips'
swerving shot from the half-way line, against Fulham in 1995. Also in
the running was Fred Binney, who beat four men before finding the
net against Rochdale in 1968, Graham Rees, shrugging off Nobby Stiles
to level the scores in a League Cup tie against Manchester United in
1960, and 'Happy' Houghton's 1931 goal in the FA Cup quarter-final
draw at Sunderland. Commenting on the winner was Exeter City
historian Mike Blackstone: 'Who needs bloody David Beckham, eh!'*

EXETER CITY 5 TORQUAY UNITED 0
THIRD DIVISION (SOUTH), 28 JANUARY 1933
(ATTENDANCE 9,591)

City (2-3-5): Arthur Davies; Jim Gray, Charlie Miller; Reg Clarke, Arthur Childs, Stan Barber; Jack Scott, John Kennedy, Fred Whitlow, Harry 'Happy' Houghton, Andy Higgins; Manager: Billy McDevitt.
United (2-3-5): Percy Maggs; Jack Fowler, Lew Tapp; Ted Anderson, Fred Martin, Tom Robinson; Ralph Birkett, Jack Tennant, George Stabb, Albert Orr, Don 'Dickie' Bird; Manager: Frank Brown.

Fred Whitlow's hat-trick in this derby took City to the top of the Third Division (South), and equalled Fred Dent's individual scoring record of 26 goals in a season for City, set in 1928. In a game where the Torquay defence were over-run, only the outstanding display of 'keeper Percy Maggs stopped the Grecians from trouncing their opponents by an even greater margin of victory.

At St James Park, the frost-bound pitch was covered in sand but the match was played in bright sunshine and, after losing the toss, the visitors kicked off facing the sun. United pressed hard for an early advantage with centre forward George Stabb and future England winger Ralph Birkett creating good chances. The tide turned when Whitlow played a ball out on the right to Jack Scott. The United defence hesitated fatally, waiting for an offside decision that never came. This allowed the winger to centre to 'Happy' Houghton, whose header rebounded off the crossbar and, in the resultant scramble, Whitlow poked the ball over the line. A further defensive lapse allowed Andy Higgins time and space to pick his spot for City's second goal. John Kennedy put the home side further ahead with a flashing diagonal shot, which one reporter claimed was one of the best ever seen at St James Park. A minute later, Whitlow added to his tally. A cross-field ball was played out wide to Scott whose first-time cross was met by Fred, who then thundered a shot against the underside of the bar. Despite desperate attempts by the United full-backs, Fowler and Tapp, to clear, the ball eluded them before nestling in the back of the net.

Four down at the interval, United came under immediate pressure after the restart, and Maggs thwarted the City forwards with a series of breathtaking saves. However, the goalkeeper's brilliance could not prevent Fred Whitlow from collecting his sixth hat-trick of the season. After sixty-eight minutes, the striker linked with Houghton, whose excellent work deceived the defence and put Fred through with only Maggs to beat. As the 'keeper rushed out of his goal to narrow the angle, Fred calmly side-stepped him and put the ball into an empty net. As he trotted back nonchalantly to the centre-circle, he received a tremendous ovation from the Grecian fans.

Bristolian Fred had been signed for £250 from Charlton Athletic, where he had helped the London side to the championship of the Third Division (South) in 1929. Despite his amazing contribution of 33 goals in 32 League games (still

Fred Whitlow – City's record-holding scorer.

a club record) he failed to repeat this promotion success with Exeter, who finished runners-up at the end of the campaign. Fred's goal-scoring touch deserted him somewhat the following season. At the age of thirty, he moved on to pastures new with Cardiff City, and subsequently ended his career where it had begun, with non-League Barry Town.

In the 'Total Football' poll to reveal the best goals of the twentieth century, Torquay fans had no hesitation in plumping for Paul Dobson's 1987 stoppage-time equalizer against Crewe, which saved the Gulls from the 'big drop'. Honourable mentions were also given to Derek Dawkins, for his stunning League Cup strike against Spurs in 1987; the fastest-ever own goal by Pat Kruse, in a League game against Cambridge in 1976, and goalkeeper Gareth Howells' sudden-death winning penalty against Blackpool in the 1991 Wembley play-off final. Gulls supporter James Penwell summed it up perfectly: 'Decades of utter crapness can make the relative successes all the sweeter.'

TORQUAY UNITED 3 EXETER CITY 1
THIRD DIVISION (SOUTH), 31 DECEMBER 1955
(ATTENDANCE 12,194)

United (2-3-5): Jimmy Kirk; John Smith, John Anderton; Dennis Lewis, Griff Norman, Norman Lloyd; Ron Shaw, Sam Collins, Jack Smith, Don Mills, Tony Collins; Manager: Eric Webber.
City (2-3-5): George Hunter; Les Doyle, Arnold Mitchell; Fred Davey, Keith Harvey, Tom Dunne; Roy Whiteside, Ray John, Ray Iggleden, Eddie Murphy, Graham Rees; Manager: Norman Dodgin.

On New Year's Eve, Plainmoor's biggest crowd of the season witnessed goal-machine Sam Collins collect his 25th League goal in 26 games and United's first hat-trick in a derby League game. In keeping with the festive season, the game was played in excellent spirit, with both sides committed to good football.

United winger Ron Shaw gave the City captain Arnold Mitchell a torrid time in the opening exchanges and seemed to have put the home side ahead, until the goal was disallowed for an infringement. However, this was a temporary respite for the Grecians. In the fourteenth minute, Jack Smith worked the ball cleverly down the middle to put Sam Collins through for his first goal. Following a good save by Hunter from Shaw, the goalkeeper palmed out a centre from left-winger Tony Collins, and Sam (no relation) was on hand to head into an unguarded net after thirty-six minutes. At this point, Torquay eased off and allowed Exeter back into the game. It was no surprise when Ray Iggleden pulled one back just before the interval. The goal was a beauty, the centre forward latching onto a cross from Graham Rees and hitting it first time into the roof of the net.

This goal obviously stung United, who started off the second half in whirlwind style, and Sam Collins completed his hat-trick within a minute of the kick-off without a City player touching the ball. Jack Smith played the ball to Don Mills from the centre-circle. 'The Don' passed the ball out to Shaw, who raced past Mitchell and crossed the ball perfectly to Smith, who arrived in the penalty area to glance the ball down to the feet of Collins, who needed no second invitation to slam the ball into the net. With City centre half Keith Harvey the pick of an overworked defence, United wasted many opportunities to increase their lead. Jack Smith had scored in the four previous League games, and the former Liverpool forward came closest to adding to the tally. His fine header was brilliantly saved just before the end by 'Flying Scot' George Hunter, who had previously won a Cup Winners' medal with Celtic.

Sam Collins went on to eclipse Jimmy Trotter's individual goal-scoring record of 28 goals in a season for Torquay – which had been set twenty-five years earlier in 1931. By the season's end, Sam had raised this total to 42 League and FA Cup goals. Released on a free transfer by Bristol City in 1948, Sam amassed 219 goals from 379 senior appearances for United and was leading scorer for

Sam Collins looks at his scrapbook of soccer memories.

seven consecutive seasons, until injury forced his retirement after ten prolific years in 1958. He left the game to run a newsagents near the Plainmoor ground for many years before retiring to his home city of Bristol. His individual and collective goal-scoring achievements were approached in the 1960s by goal legend Robin Stubbs, but they still stand and it appears increasingly unlikely that they will ever be broken.

Plymouth Argyle were trounced 6-4 at Charlton on Boxing Day 1960, then amazingly won the return the following day at Home Park by the same margin, with Wilf Carter setting an individual scoring record by netting five times! Exeter City travelled to Brighton on Christmas Day 1946 and won 6-1, with centre forward Bill Owen, who had started the season at wing-half, scoring a hat-trick. Torquay United entertained Crystal Palace on Christmas Day 1934 and handed out a 7-1 thrashing, with Albert Hutchinson collecting a hat-trick! The following year, the Magpies gave the home fans another unexpected Christmas present by beating Newport County 6-1, which included a Ted Lowery hat-trick!

EXETER CITY 4 PLYMOUTH ARGYLE 2
THIRD DIVISION (SOUTH), 8 FEBRUARY 1958
(ATTENDANCE 13,958)

City (2-3-5): George Hunter; Norman Packer, Les MacDonald; Ray John, Nelson Stiffle, Arnold Mitchell; Graham Rees, Dennis Churms, Ted Calland, Johnny Nichols, Gordon Dale; Manager: Bill Thompson.
Argyle (2-3-5): Geoff Barnsley; George Robertson, John Timmins; Johnny Williams, Reg Wyatt, Rex Tilley; Harry Penk, Wilf Carter, George Baker, Jimmy Gauld, Peter Anderson; Manager: Jack Rowley.

In 1954, Johnny Nicholls had the soccer world at his feet. On his twenty-third birthday, he scored on his debut for England, then a month later won an FA Cup winners medal with West Bromwich Albion, where he formed a lethal striking partnership with fellow international Ronnie Allen. His meteoric rise to the top was equalled by a downward spiral into mediocrity. At a time when he could have been expected to be approaching his peak, his poaching skills inexplicably lost their edge and he was replaced by another England prospect, Derek Kevan. Moving on to Second Division side Cardiff in May 1957, he made only a handful of appearances before arriving at St James Park six months later for a fee of £4,500. A shadow of the player that had starred at the Hawthorns, Johnny still showed occasional touches of class, particularly in this performance against Argyle.

Before the game, both teams lined up and the crowd stood in silence, as a mark of respect to the memory of the 'Busby Babes' who had perished two days earlier in the

John Nichols showed the class that had won him top honours.

Munich disaster. Plymouth had gone nine League games without defeat and were pushing hard for the championship, while Exeter were lying at the foot of the table. Not unusually, form was turned upside down in a local derby. The treacherous pitch also played its part. It was totally unsuited to Argyle's short-passing game, which came to grief in the clinging mud, and they failed to utilise the wings, where the surface was better. Yet, all seemed set fair for Argyle's first post-war win at St James Park when Harry Penk shot them into a twenty-fourth minute lead with a fierce drive which went in off a post. They clung onto their advantage for only ten minutes before Nicholls nipped in for the equaliser. Linking well with centre forward Ted Calland, Johnny scored again from close range soon after the break and collected his hat-trick with all his old aplomb after sixty-seven minutes. Argyle stormed back into the game with a goal from Jimmy Gauld, but any hopes of salvaging a point were dashed when a controversial penalty was awarded near the close. Reg Wyatt was adjudged to have brought down Nicholls and, although the decision appeared harsh, Arnold Mitchell converted the spot-kick to put the game beyond the visitors' reach.

This loss may have cost Plymouth a place in the Second Division, for in the final analysis they missed promotion by two points. City finished bottom of the table, but were saved from re-election when the Football League was reconstructed to abandon the regional divisions. The Grecians started the following season as founder members of the Fourth Division. Therefore, Johnny Nicholls completed a nap hand, playing in all four divisions in the space of three seasons. Recovering from a knee injury, which required surgery, his form remained inconsistent and he was allowed to move to non League Worcester City. At the age of twenty-eight, a once glittering career was over.

Many sons have followed in their father's footsteps and turned out for Devon soccer clubs. Bob Jack became Argyle's first professional in 1903, and was their longest-serving manager. His three sons – David, Rollo and Donald – were all on the club's books. Robert Swiggs turned out for Argyle in the 1950s, and son Bradley did likewise thirty years later. Sam Shilton made his League debut for Plymouth in 1994, while his father, Peter, was manager. Bill Harrower played for Torquay and Exeter in the immediate postwar period, and his son, Stephen, joined The Grecians in the 1980s. Barry Redwood's promising career with Exeter was brought to a premature end by injury in 1963, and his son, Toby, made his bow for City in 1990. Torquay United signed former England winger Dave Mercer in 1929, and his son, Dave Junior, appeared for the Magpies, just after the Second World War. In the late 1970s, Maurice Cox and Stuart Clarke, brought back memories of their fathers, Geoff Cox and Doug Clarke, who had graced Plainmoor a decade earlier. Fifteen years after his last appearance for the Gulls, Cliff Myers watched his son Chris step out at Wembley for United in 1991. Chris also played for Exeter. West Ham's Ken Brown and John Bond moved to Torquay in the 1960s. Their sons, Kenny and Kevin, turned out for Plymouth and Exeter respectively.

EXETER CITY 0 TORQUAY UNITED 3
FOURTH DIVISION, 18 AUGUST 1962,
(ATTENDANCE 9,676)

City (2-3-5): Colin Tinsley; Dave Johnston, Les MacDonald; Arnold Mitchell, Des Anderson, Mike Hughes; Ray Carter, Charlie Sells, Barry Pierce, Eric Welsh, Reg Jenkins; Manager; Cyril Spiers.

United (2-3-5): Terry Adlington; John Rossiter, George Allen; Geoff Cox, Colin Bettany, Dave Hancock; Gordon Astall, Bobby Webb, Tommy Northcott, Brian Handley, Ernie Pym; Manager; Eric Webber.

There were two international-class wingers on view in this match: United's former Plymouth, Birmingham and England player, Gordon Astall, and City's Eric Welsh, a future Northern Ireland cap with Carlisle, who was also destined to join Torquay towards the end his League career. Both men were outshone on this occasion by another winger, Ernie Pym, whose hat-trick was the first scored for an away team in a local League derby.

Torquay United had been relegated the previous season after just two campaigns in the Third Division, but in this opening match back in the basement they completely outplayed their Devon neighbours. This did not seem possible during the first twenty minutes, when it was all Exeter. The

Ernie Pym – goal-scoring winger.

Grecians should have exploited huge gaps in the United defence and Charlie Sells and Ray Carter had shots which narrowly missed the target, before Barry Pierce hit an upright with a header. United rode out the storm and the tide turned in their favour with a slice of outrageous fortune. City centre half Des Anderson attempted a clearance, which slammed against the body of the onrushing Ernie Pym and rebounded past the astonished home 'keeper Colin Tinsley.

From that moment on, United never looked in trouble and took complete control of the match. The first may have been a fluke but the second was sheer class. Ernie collected the ball on the half-way line and, with a tremendous burst of speed, outstripped the defence, took the ball almost to the byline and then unleashed an amazing shot which found the net from an impossible-looking angle.

Torquay continued to dominate in the second half and Pym sealed the result, as well as collecting his third goal of the afternoon, when he cut inside to chase a long ball down the middle from Tommy Northcott. The City defence were caught flat-footed and the diminutive winger raced through before gleefully lashing the ball into the net from close range. An overworked home defence battled manfully to subdue a rampant United attack, with Arnold Mitchell and Les McDonald performing wonders to prevent further goals.

Ernie Pym had joined his hometown club in 1957 from local side St Marychurch Spurs. Scouts were often in evidence running the rule over him at Plainmoor, as his consistent goal-scoring feats attracted the attention of the bigger clubs. However, he remained a one-club man, scoring 94 goals in 307 appearances. The first hat-trick of his career came in United's club record 7-1 FA Cup win over Northampton in the 1959/60 season, when he was a prominent member of the side which won promotion to the Third Division.

Argyle's 'Gentleman George' Dews and Barry Meyer fulfilled every schoolboy's dream in the 1950s by playing professional soccer in the winter and county cricket in the summer. Team-mates 'Jumbo' Chisholm and Bill Strauss were also excellent cricketers and represented minor counties. Torquay's Don Welsh, in the 1930s, and Brian Handley, in the 1960s, were also club professionals with Torbay cricket teams. Great things were obviously expected of Exeter's Barnsley-born defender Hedley Verity Steele – who was named after the great Yorkshire and England spin bowler, who lost his life in the Second World War.

PLYMOUTH ARGYLE 6 TORQUAY UNITED 0
THIRD DIVISION 26 DECEMBER 1969,
(ATTENDANCE 17,128)

Argyle (4-3-3): Martin Clamp; John Hore, David Lean, Winston Foster, Colin Sullivan; Norman Piper, Steve Davey, Aiden Mather; Richard Reynolds, Derek Rickard, Mike Bickle; Sub: Trevor Shepherd; Manager: Billy Bingham.
United (4-2-4): Andy Donnelly; Cecil Smyth, Jimmy Dunne, Bill Kitchener, Brian Joy; Tommy Mitchinson, Mickey Cave; Eric Welsh, Alan Welsh, John Rudge (sub: John Benson), Tony Scott; Manager: Allan Brown.

This result was one Christmas present which came as a seasonal surprise, even to the most green-eyed Argyle fans. They witnessed a remarkable transformation in a team which was floundering in the bottom half of the table and had not registered a League win for six games. By contrast, United fans were left wondering how a team that had already knocked Plymouth out of the Football League Cup, could tamely surrender a current League run of eight consecutive draws. The answer lay mainly in the amount of freedom given to Norman Piper,who played a part in all the goals. He loaded the ammunition and four-goal striker Mike Bickle fired the bullets that gunned down the Gulls in this Boxing Day massacre.

Piper opened the scoring with a twenty-sixth minute penalty and ten minutes later created an opening which was converted brilliantly by Mike Bickle, who ended a barren spell of four games without a goal to put Argyle two up at the break. Before United could play themselves back into the match, Bickle slammed in two more chances to notch up his hat-trick after an hour's play. Twenty minutes later, Norman Piper contemptuously stroked home a free-kick which Pele would have been proud of. Just before the close, a devastating exhibition of fire-power was completed by Bickle who, for the second time in his career, became a four-goal hero for Argyle. On the first occasion, Cardiff had been the team to suffer. This time, the Torquay team had been stuffed like a Christmas turkey, and they trooped off the pitch to be 'roasted' by their new manager, Allan Brown. It had been a baptism of fire for Brown, who had just taken over the reins of one of United's most successful teams from Frank O'Farrell, who had accepted the challenge of trying to save First Division side Leicester City from relegation. Frank had earlier turned down overtures from Home Park and recommended Billy Bingham for the job. After this amazing derby result, the Argyle manager was left believing that perhaps there was a Santa Claus after all!

Sports editors dubbed Mike Bickle 'The Fastest Milkman in the West', as the former Co-operative Society delivery-man tore through opposition defences. Eight goals in six reserve games convinced Argyle to sign the striker in December 1965. Establishing himself in the first team the following season, he became the club's leading marksman during four consecutive League

*Mike Bickle – Fastest
Milkman in the West!*

campaigns. After scoring 74 goals in 196 senior appearances for Argyle, he moved on to Gillingham in November 1971. Soon however, injury problems brought about his retirement from the game. He remains the only player to score four goals in a League derby, having inflicted the heaviest drubbing on Torquay in 28 League meetings between the two clubs.

When the joint tenants of Plainmoor, Babbacombe and Torquay Town, discussed the possibility of merging and turning professional in 1921, they were encouraged by directors of Exeter City, who attended a meeting of interested parties and offered to become shareholders in the newly-formed Torquay United. Six years later, their confidence was justified, as United had been transformed into a fully-fledged League club. However, trouble was around the corner, and the Magpies nearly went out of business in January 1930, when the grandstand roof was blown off in severe gales. In debt with the bank, and unable to meet the costs of reconstruction, the club was saved from extinction when rivals Exeter City and Plymouth Argyle came to their aid by generously offering to take part in friendly fund-raising matches at Plainmoor!

EXETER CITY 4 TORQUAY UNITED 3
DIVISION FOUR, 26 DECEMBER 1984
(ATTENDANCE 3,925)

City (4-4-2): Jeff Wood; Phil Coleman, Nicky Marker, Jim McNichol, Keith Viney; Dan O'Shea, Martin Ling, Kevin Smith (sub: Steve Harrower), Ian Davies; Trevor Morgan, Ray Pratt; Manager: Jim Iley.
United (4-4-2): Kenny Allen; Doug McClure, Derek Fowler, John Impey (sub: Steve Pugh), Colin Anderson; Andy Best, Derek Hall, Derek Dawkins, Gary Marshall; Benny Laryea, John Sims; Manager: Bruce Rioch.

Before the match, the Exeter faithful were handed Christmas cards produced by director Dan McCauley, who earlier in the month had unsuccessfully offered £100,000 to buy out all the shareholders and guarantee Exeter's debts. To the amusement of fans conditioned to supporting a team in the lower reaches of the League, Mr McCauley promised that he would 'get the club back to where it belongs'. In a personal message to supporters, he urged them to boycott future matches to put financial pressure on the board. However, the type of vintage soccer entertainment produced in this Boxing Day clash was just what was required to bring the crowds back, not persuade them to stay away!

After a dozen games without a win, the match proved to be lucky thirteen for the Grecians. In the first League meeting of the old rivals for seven years, City snatched victory in a nail-biting finish, thanks to a Ray Pratt hat-trick. The Gulls played their part in a pulsating match, but the result left them languishing at the foot of the table, where they were to remain until the end of the season. With twenty minutes to go, the result did not appear in doubt, as City were leading 3-0 and seemingly cruising to victory.

Within two minutes, Exeter had taken the lead, when Ray Pratt scored with a diving header following a corner. After half an hour, Kevin Smith added a second with a powerful drive and in stoppage time, Pratt stabbed the ball home from close range to give the Grecians what should have been an unassailable lead. United had other ideas, however, and took the game to the opposition after the interval. The pressure finally brought some reward in the seventy-first minute, when Gary Mason embarrassed 'keeper Jeff Wood by curling a corner straight into the net. Two minutes later, Derek Hall reduced the arrears further with a tremendous 30-yard drive into the top corner of the net. Panic set into the City defence and United took full advantage of the situation, continuing a stirring fightback with their third goal in six minutes. A Gary Marshall free-kick dropped to Derek Hall, whose shot was blocked before rebounding to John Sims. The former City striker calmly stabbed in the equaliser to tremendous acclaim from United supporters.

Grecian fans feared the worst, and would not have been surprised if the Gulls had gone on to snatch victory. Instead, Exeter recovered their composure and, with only nine minutes to go, Martin Ling swung in a corner which was flicked

Ray Pratt – Player of the Year.

on by Trevor Morgan to Ray Pratt. The Welsh striker made no mistake, chalking up his second hat-trick of the season. Ray went on to be voted Player of the Year, despite an ankle injury curtailing his season. He never fully recovered from this setback, however, and made only a handful of appearances the following season before his playing days came to an end.

David and Rollo Jack were the first brothers to play for Plymouth Argyle in the early 1920s. Bob and Dave Thomas turned out for Argyle immediately after the Second World War, and Neil and Peter Langman were influential members of the side during the 1950s. Brothers who have given sterling postwar service to Torquay United are the three Callands, Ralph, Albert and Ted; Jack and Alan Smith; Tommy and George Northcott; Ken and Phil Sandercock. Ted Calland and George Northcott also played for Exeter. Other siblings with different allegiances include Jason and Darren Rowbotham, who began their careers at Plymouth before Darren moved on to Torquay and Exeter. Bruce and Neil Rioch played for Torquay and Plymouth respectively, and, likewise, John Sharpe turned out for Exeter, while his famous brother Lee started at Torquay, before becoming an England international with Manchester United.

PLYMOUTH ARGYLE 4 TORQUAY UNITED 3
DIVISION THREE, 21 OCTOBER 1995
(ATTENDANCE 11, 695)

Argyle (4-3-3): Kevin Blackwell; Mark Patterson, Mick Heathcote, Keith Hill, Paul Williams; Martin Barlow (Kevin McGee 45 mins), Ronnie Mauge, Chris Leadbitter (sub: Gary Clayton); Mickey Evans, Ian Baird, Adrian Littlejohn. United (5-2-3): Ashley Bayes; Chris Curran, Lee Barrow, Don O'Riordan (sub: Ellis Laight), Ian Gore, Tom Kelly; Mark Hawthorne, Russell Coughlin; Rodney Jack, Jamie Ndah (sub: Kevin Hodges), Scott Partridge; Manager: Don O'Riordan.

Argyle and United's first League meeting for twenty-four years produced a classic encounter between two sides at opposite ends of the table. In their previous League game, United had been badly beaten 4-0 at home by Preston, and even the most ardent of Gulls fans could not have been optimistic about the outcome at Home Park. Yet, Torquay's stirring performance came so close to upsetting the form book and denting Plymouth's promotion challenge. The difference between the sides proved to be £100,000 summer capture Adrian Littlejohn. The former England youth international notched his ninth goal in nine games for the Greens, and rattled in the first hat-trick of his career to clinch victory five minutes from time.

Adrian Littlejohn poses a threat at the near post.

Argyle took an early lead when Littlejohn burst into the penalty area and held off a challenge from Lee Barrow, before driving in a shot to the far post. Prompted by manager Don O'Riordan, dictating play from the sweeper position, United hit back with an equaliser from Jamie Ndah, who stooped to head in a chance created by the effervescent Rodney Jack. In the twenty-third minute, the Gulls deservedly took the lead when O'Riordan found Russell Coughlin on the right. The former Argyle and Exeter schemer volleyed the ball into the goalmouth, where Ndah stabbed the ball past 'keeper Kevin Blackwell. The action swept from end to end before Argyle levelled the scores in the thirty-seventh minute with a goal that looked suspiciously offside. Chris Leadbitter was running through with the ball until stumbling; quick as a flash, Littlejohn seized onto the ball and fired home from the edge of the area. Five minutes before the break, Torquay forged ahead once again, when Scott Partridge cut inside from the left-hand side of the area and hit a tremendous drive into the top right-hand corner.

After the interval, the whole pattern of the game changed when United skipper Ian Gore was sent-off for his second bookable offence in the sixty-fourth minute. Ten-man Torquay held out for fifteen minutes before Ronnie Mauge, unmarked at the far post, brought Argyle back into the match. The scene was now set for Adrian Littlejohn to complete a treble of left-foot strikes, which finally broke Torquay's resistance. Unbelievably, in the next match at Plainmoor, United capitulated 1-8 to Scunthorpe, Don O'Riordan was sacked and the team finished bottom of the League.

Adrian Littlejohn's 19 League goals helped Argyle to Wembley glory, when they were promoted after a play-off final against Darlington. Two seasons later, as Argyle were heading for relegation, Littlejohn found himself utilised as an emergency left-back, and he became increasingly unhappy before joining Oldham in March 1998.

In soccer's often farcical game of musical chairs, managers who remain with the same club for three years surely qualify for a long-service medal! Each of the Devon clubs has had a manager, who has surpassed this modest target and taken it well into double figures. Argyle's first professional player, Robert Jack, had two spells as manager, including an unbroken run of twenty-eight years from 1910-1938. Torquay's Eric Webber took over initially as player-manager, on the day Winston Churchill was returned to power in October 1951, and lasted nearly fourteen years, until relieved of his post in May 1965. Former England international Arthur Chadwick also spent fourteen years in charge of Exeter in a period interrupted by war, from 1908-1922. He left the club to manage Clapton Orient and died in the stand at St James Park whilst watching his two former clubs play a League match in March 1936.

TORQUAY UNITED 0 PLYMOUTH ARGYLE 4
DIVISION THREE, 25 MARCH 2000
(ATTENDANCE 4,113)

United (5-3-2): Stuart Jones; Paul Holmes, Wayne Thomas, Alex Watson, Lee Russell, Robbie Herrera; Chris Brandon, Brian Healey, Kevin Hill; Tony Bedeau (sub: Mike Griffiths), Eifion Williams; Manager: Wes Saunders.
Argyle (3-5-2): Jon Sheffield; Craig Taylor, Jason Rowbotham, Adam Barrett; Wayne O'Sullivan, Craig Etherington, Paul Wotton, Chris Hargreaves, Jon Beswetherick; Paul McGregor (sub: Martin Gritton), Steve Guinan (sub: Sean McCarthy); Manager: Kevin Hodges.

Leading marksman Paul McGregor, who had failed to find the net in six previous outings, rediscovered his goal-scoring touch with a triple strike which enabled Argyle to achieve their best-ever League win at Plainmoor. Any illusions that United may have supplanted Plymouth as Devon's leading team were destroyed, as this shock result was a severe setback to the Gulls' promotion hopes. In midweek, United had beaten title contenders Darlington, now with eight games remaining, the Greens convincingly leapfrogged over their neighbours and moved up the table to give themselves a realistic chance of clinching a play-off spot.

Bright sunshine gave way to a hailstorm at the outset of the match, the pools of water that had formed on the ground leaving it resembling a paddy field. Indications that this was not going to be United's day occurred in the twenty-second minute, when top scorer Tony Bedeau was carried off with a twisted ankle. A minute later, McGregor back-heeled the ball to Jon Beswetherwick on the right-hand edge of the area. The wing-back swung over a pinpoint centre for skipper Craig Taylor to head Plymouth into the lead. After half an hour's play, 'keeper Stuart Jones hesitated to meet a low cross from Beswetherick, allowing Paul McGregor to nip in and sweep the ball past him for the first leg of his hat-trick.

Either side of the interval, United desperately tried to haul themselves back into the match, but Plymouth's defence proved equal to the task. With Jon Beswetherick exploiting space and causing endless problems down the left flank, it was no surprise when Torquay's resistance was broken again in the seventy-first minute. A surging run from Beswetherick took him past Paul Holmes and, cutting into the box, he drew the 'keeper, before sliding the ball to an unmarked McGregor, who side-footed the ball into an unguarded net. McGregor's third goal came seven minutes later. The flag stayed down as he ran onto a through ball from Chris Hargreaves. As Jones advanced to narrow the angle, he was deliberately 'nutmegged' as the striker cheekily pushed the ball into the net through his legs!

Paul McGregor became only the eleventh striker to score a hat-trick in a Devon League derby. He was voted Man of the Match by the sponsors, an award normally reserved for a home player. His performance also left him £100 richer, as he collected a bet from manager Kevin Hodges, having passed a target of 10 League goals for the season. Predictably, Argyle's promotion hopes quickly evaporated, and they were overtaken in the League table by the Gulls, who squandered a golden opportunity to reach the play-offs by losing their last game at home to Northampton.

Paul McGregor celebrates his first goal, after capitalizing on a mistake by 'keeper Stuart Jones, who holds his head in anguish.

STATISTICS
Devon's Leading League Scorers

	Plymouth Argyle	Exeter City	Torquay United
1920/21	Harry Raymond 7	C. Vowles/B. Wright 9	-
1921/22	Frank Richardson 31	Charlie Vowles 11	-
1922/23	Jack Fowler 17	Harry Crockford 17	-
1923/24	Percy Cherrett 27	Harry Kirk 8	-
1924/25	Jack Leslie 14	Harry Kirk 12	-
1925/26	Jack Cock 31	Wilf Lievesley 18	-
1926/27	Jack Cock 33	Harold Blackmore 25	-
1927/28	Sammy Black 16	Frank Dent 26	Bert Turner 11
1928/29	Ray Bowden 21	Ed Cameron 9	Cyrill Hemingway 11
1929/30	Sammy Black 21	Cyril Hemingway 19	Joe Pointon 18
1930/31	Sammy Black 20	Paercy Varco 25	Jimmy Trotter 26
1931/32	Jack Leslie 20	P. Varco/H. Houghton 16	Bill Clayson 14
1932/33	Sammy Black 13	Fred Whitlow 33	George Stabb 24
1933/34	Jimmy Cookson 27	Stan Hurst 14	Frank Ryder 9
1934/35	Jack Vidler 21	Poulter/F. Wrightson 16	Albert Hutchinson 18
1935/36	Sammy Black 15	Jim McCambridge 14	Albert Hutchinson 10
1936/37	Jack Vidler 13	Rod Williams 29	Ben Morton 23
1937/38	Bill Hullett 10	Harry Bowl 18	Ben Morton 10
1938/39	Bill Hullett 10	Harry Bowl 24	Ralph Allen 15
1946/47	Dave Thomas 19	Digger Ebdon 16	Jack Conley 23
1947/48	Ernire Edds 14	Duggie Regan 11	Ron Shaw 17
1948/49	Maurice Tadman 15	Duggie Regan 14	Jack Conley 19
1949/50	Bill Strauss 10	Richard Smart 13	Jack Conley 14
1950/51	Maurice Tadman 23	Archie Smith 22	R. Shaw/S. Collins 11
1951/52	Maurice Tadman 27	Aungus MacKay 20	E. Edds/S. Collins 22
1952/53	Maurice Tadman 15	Jim Dailey 13	Sam Collins 27
1953/54	Maurice Tadman 11	Charlie MaClelland 19	Sam Collins 17
1954/55	Porteous/Davis/Anderson 8	Charlie McClelland 9	Sam Collins 26
1955/56	Neil Langman 9	Ron Burke 10	Sam Collins 40
1956/57	Neil Langman 17	Jim Currie 14	Sam Collins 30
1957/58	Wilf Carter 26	Ted Calland 15	Tommy Northcott 13
1958/59	Wilf Carter 22	Ted Calland 27	Tommy Northcott 20
1959/60	Wilf Carter 22	Graham Rees 17	Tommy Northcott 15
1960/61	Wilf Carter 24	Graham Rees 14	Tommy Northcott 26
1961/62	Wilf Carter 19	Ray Carter 19	Ernie Pym 19
1962/63	Wilf Carter 14	Ray Carter 19	Brian Handley 20
1963/64	Frank Lord 8	Alan Banks 18	Robin Stubbs 24
1964/65	Mike Trebilcock 15	Dermot Curtis 9	Robin Stubbs 31
1965/66	Mike Trebilcock 11	Alan Banks 17	Tommy Spratt 18
1966/67	Mike Bickle 13	Dixie McNeil 11	Robin Stubbs 21
1967/68	Mike Bickle 10	John Corr 7	Robin Stubbs 9
1968/69	Mike Bickle 12	Alan Banks 13	Robin Stubbs 18
1969/70	Mike Bickle 18	Joe Gadston 10	Alan Welsh 10
1970/71	Denis Hutchins 11	Alan Banks 21	John Rudge 17
1971/72	Derek Rickard 14	Fred Binney 28	Alan Welsh 10
1972/73	Alan Welsh 12	Fred Binney 25	Mike Trebilcock 10
1973/74	Paul Mariner 14	Fred Binney 25	Eddie Rowles 10
1974/75	Bill Rafferty 23	Keith Bowker 18	Cliff Myers 8
1975/76	Paul Mariner 15	Alan Beer 20	Willie Brown 14
1976/77	Brian Hall 10	Alan Beer 20	Willie Brown 18
1977/78	Terry Austin 11	Tony Kellow 14	Willie Brown 12
1978/79	Fred Binney 26	Keith Bowker 11	Les Lawrence 17
1979/80	Dave Kemp 15	Dave Pullar 10	Steve Cooper 17
1980/81	Dave Kemp 24	Tony Kellow 25	Gerry Fell 12
1981/82	John Sims 18	Tony Kellow 21	Tony Brown 11
1982/83	Kevin Hodges 11	Steve Neville 17	Steve Cooper 15
1983/84	Tommy Tynan 12	Ray Pratt 16	Cooper/Sims/Barnes 8
1984/85	Tommy Tynan 31	Ray Pratt 20	Mario Walsh 5
1985/86	Kevin Hodges 16	Tony Kellow 9	Steve Phillips 8
1986/87	Tommy Tynan 18	Tony Kellow 15	Paul Dobson 9
1987/88	Tommy Tynan 16	Dean Edwards 12	Paul Dobson 22
1988/89	Tommy Tynan 24	Darren Rowbotham 20	Dean Edwards 8
1989/90	Tommy Tynan 15	Darren Rowbotham 20	Mark Loram 12
1990/91	Robbie Turner 14	S. Neville/M. Cooper 11	Dean Edwards 15
1991/92	Dwight Marshall 14	Steve Moran 19	John Fashanu 10
1992/93	S. Castle/K Nugent 11	John Hodge 15	Duane Darby 12
1993/94	Steve Castle 21	Ronnie Jepson 13	Adrian Foster 15
1994/95	R Landon/K Nugent 7	Mike Cecere 10	Richard Hancox 9
1995/96	Adrian Littlejohn 17	Mark Cooper 6	P. Baker/P. Buckle 4
1996/97	Mickey Evans 12	Darren Rowbotham 9	Rodney Jack 10
1997/98	Carlo Corazzin 16	Darren Rowbotham 20	Rodney Jack 12
1998/99	Dwight Marshall 12	Steve Flack 11	Scott Partridge 12
1999/2000	Paul McGregor 16	Garry Alexander 16	Tony Bedeau 16
2000/01	Paul McGregor 13	Steve Flack 13	K. Hill/E. Williams 9

3
CUP CLASHES

Argyle boss Neil Warnock and City manager Peter Fox, as depicted by cartoonist Tom before the FA Cup derby in 1996.

TORQUAY UNITED 0 EXETER CITY 1
FA CUP SECOND ROUND, 8 DECEMBER 1928,
(ATTENDANCE 8,425)

United (2-3-5): Harold Gough, Jack Fowler, Bill Brown; Arthur Smeaton, Jim Carrick, Bob Smith; Jim Mackey, Dan Kelly, Wally Gardner, Cyril Hemingway, Harry Waller; Manager: Percy Mackrill.
City: (2-3-5): Tom Holland; Wilf Lowton, Charlie Miller; Bob Pollard, Alex Pool, Reg 'Nobby' Clarke; George Purcell, Billy McDevitt, Arthur Doncaster, Harry 'Happy' Houghton, Bill Death; Manager: David Wilson.

A record crowd attended Plainmoor to witness Torquay United and Exeter City's first meeting in the FA Cup. Each set of supporters also had their own marching band to cheer, as they were entertained by both the Torquay Brass Band and the Exeter City Military Band before the kick-off. United had recorded a convincing home League win against their neighbours earlier in the season, and were confident of making further progress in the competition. The Magpies' captain Harold Gough won the toss and City found themselves facing bright sunshine in the first half. The advantage counted for nothing, as the Grecians set about their rivals with a vengeance. United were never allowed time to settle as their opponents battled for every ball.

The intensity of City's challenges resulted in the Torquay trainer rushing on to administer the 'magic sponge' to three injured players. Wally Gardner received a nasty cut above the eye, while Cyril Hemingway and Harry Carrick both also required attention – the latter's leg injury eventually forced him to limp off ten minutes from the end. Yet, despite Exeter's robust tackling, it was United who were penalised when left-back Bill Brown brought down Arthur Doncaster in the area, shortly before the interval. The Grecians missed a golden opportunity to take the lead when Wilf Lowton blazed his spot-kick against the inside of the upright. To the relief of the home fans, the ball flew along the line behind the 'keeper and went harmlessly out of play on the far touchline.

Exeter grew in confidence during the second period, and Magpie supporters agreed that this was their team's worst performance of the season. The home team failed to match the Grecians' ferocious application and pace. Only the brilliance of former England 'keeper Harold Gough kept United in the game, as he denied the City forwards time and again. Ironically, it was a defensive error which presented Exeter with a well-deserved winner twelve minutes from time. Bill Death raced down the left touchline and passed inside to Nobby Clarke. The wing-half crossed the ball into the box, where the unfortunate Bill Brown had time to clear the danger at the far post. Instead, he attempted to head back to the 'keeper and the ball fell invitingly at the feet of winger George Purcell, who took full advantage by slamming the ball into the roof of the net past a powerless Gough.

Left: *George Purcell scores the winner.* Right: *United's skipper Harold Gough made some brilliant saves.*

Torquay rallied strongly, but wily Exeter skipper Billy McDevitt waved everyone back behind the ball and two goal-bound efforts rebounded off a packed defence. City hung onto their slender lead and booked a place in the third round for the third consecutive season, where they were defeated after a replay by First Division side Leeds United.

EXETER CITY 1 TORQUAY 0
THIRD DIVISION (SOUTH) CHALLENGE CUP FINAL, 2 MAY 1934
(ATTENDANCE 6,198)

City (2-3-5): Arthur Chesters; Jimmy Gray, Charlie Miller; Reg 'Nobby' Clarke, Harold Webb, Jack Angus; Jack Scott, Henry Poulter, Stan Hurst, Fred Wrightson, John Barnes; Manager: Billy McDevitt.
United (2-3-5): Percy Maggs; Evan Rees, Lew Tapp; Les Lievesley, Don Welsh, Tommy Pickersgill; Ernie Steele, Jack Kennedy, Fred Flavell, Albert Hutchinson, 'Dickie' Bird; Manager: Frank Brown.

A solitary goal, scored thirty minutes from time, gave Exeter City the distinction of becoming the first holders of this prestigious challenge trophy for teams in Third Division (South). Torquay had received a first-round bye, before easing past Charlton Athletic at home and Aldershot away to reach the semi-final. A convincing 4-1 win at Highbury over Third Division (South) champions-elect Norwich City swept them through to the final.

City's route in the competition was more arduous. Drawn at home for the first three rounds, the Grecians dispatched Crystal Palace with an amazing 11-6 win, eliminated Watford, and then drew with Coventry before winning the replay at Highfield Road. The semi-final against Brighton & Hove Albion at Craven Cottage resulted in stalemate. City then failed to capitalise on home advantage in the first replay before beating the Seagulls 4-3 in their own

Stan Hurst's goal secures the cup for City.

backyard. This semi-final victory set up a derby, which was played on neutral territory at Home Park. Judged on League form, mid-table City were favourites to overcome a United side struggling to avoid re-election. Surprisingly, City took the field without goal-machine Fred Whitlow, whose form had dipped after collecting six goals in the match against Crystal Palace.

There was a sensational start to the match when Torquay went all out to upset the odds. Within a minute, City centre half Harold Webb handled on the edge of the area and Fred Flavell fired home a magnificent free-kick. However, the goal was disallowed when winger Ernie Steele was adjudged to be offside. United continued to press, and 'keeper Arthur Chesters denied their attack on several occasions before his opposite number, Percy Maggs, was called upon to make a save.

The Grecians' luck held out and they showed considerable improvement in the second half. After an enterprising start, centre forward Stan Hurst eluded future England international Don Welsh, hitting the crossbar with a fierce shot before making the breakthrough a minute later. He forced a diving save from Maggs, who turned a hard drive away only as far as Jack Scott. Before the 'keeper could get to his feet, the winger turned the ball back to Hurst, who made no mistake in front of an unguarded net. Rocked by this setback, United faded as City forced the pace. Stan Hurst missed a gilt-edged chance to sew up the game ten minutes from the end when he headed over from close range with Maggs off his line. In the closing stages, Torquay fought back strongly and had their best opportunity to draw level in the last minute. Ernie Steele broke through the defence and sent in a scorching cross-shot which was brilliantly anticipated by Arthur Chesters. To the relief of the Grecians, the final whistle sounded and their skipper, Nobby Clarke, proudly stepped forward at the head of his team to receive the trophy from League representative, Louis Bellati, chairman of their vanquished first-round opponents, Crystal Palace.

Wembley Stadium's first-ever match was the FA Cup final played in April 1923 between Bolton Wanderers and West Ham. The victorious Wanderers side contained three England internationals with connections to Devon clubs. Exeter-born goalkeeper Dick Pym had been transferred from City for £5,000 in 1921, while right-winger Billy Butler later managed Torquay United at the end of the Second World War and David Jack, son of Argyle manager Robert Jack, had started his League career at Plymouth, before moving to Bolton for £3,000. Jack scored the first-ever goal at Wembley, and was in the side which also won the 1926 FA Cup final. Following his transfer to Arsenal, Wanderers replaced him with Exeter City's Harold Blackmore, who scored in the 1929 Cup Final, as The Trotters won the trophy for the third time in the 1920s.

TORQUAY UNITED 3 EXETER CITY 1
FA CUP FIRST ROUND, 26 NOVEMBER 1938
(ATTENDANCE 8,432)

United (2-3-5): Phil Joslin; Bert Head, Sid Perry; Harold Cothliff, Albert Hutchinson, Bill Coley; Arthur Rhodes, Herbert Dyer, Ralph Allen, Andy Brown, Albert James; Manager: Alf Steward.
City: Henry Church; Bill Brown, Ben Clarke; Jack Angus, Bill Fellowes, Steve Walker; Len Rich, Richard 'Digger' Ebdon, Harry Bowl, Harry Riley, Jim Liddle; Manager: Jack English.

Torquay United had already gained a League win over their derby rivals at St James Park, but their home form coming into this FA Cup encounter was far from encouraging. Since the start of the season, the Magpies had won only one of eight outings in front of their own supporters. During the opening period, the Plainmoor faithful feared the worst as Exeter played fast, open football and took an early grip on the game. City wingers, Len Rich and Jim Liddle, were a constant threat and kept goalkeeper Phil Joslin busy dealing with a flow of dangerous crosses. It was no surprise, even to the most die-hard of Magpie supporters, when the Grecians opened the scoring midway through the first half. Exeter were awarded a free-kick, which winghalf Jack Angus thundered into the goalmouth. Joslin punched the ball to the edge of the box, where Harry Riley was first to react. Latching quickly onto the ball, the inside forward drove the ball through a crowded penalty area and scored a fine goal. City continued to dominate the game and deservedly held their advantage at the interval.

The half-time pep-talk from new manager Alf Steward must have fired up United for the second half, as they looked a different team after the break. Taking the game to City, the United forward line put the away side under constant pressure and the turning point of the match came after seventy minutes. Winger Arthur Rhodes was fouled on the right flank and floated a free-kick into the penalty area. The City

A section of the crowd at Plainmoor.

defence failed to clear the danger and, following a scramble in the goalmouth, striker Andy Brown forced the ball over the line for a well-deserved equaliser. Seven minutes later, United took the lead with a superb piece of opportunism. Inside forward Ralph Allen glided past the Exeter skipper, Bill Fellowes, and drew the 'keeper. As Henry Church dived bravely at the oncoming forward's feet, Allen cleverly beat him by flicking the ball over his outstretched hands into the net. With the ecstatic home crowd now fully behind their team, City's resistance evaporated and United collected their third goal in ten minutes when Arthur Rhodes fired in from close range.

For the remainder of the match, a rampant United attack tested the City defence severely and only fine saves by Henry Church kept the

Torquay skipper Albert Hutchinson (left) shakes hands with Exeter's Bill Fellowes.

score-line respectable. On their journey home, the disgruntled Grecian army of travelling fans could only contemplate how their team had suffered such a reversal, after totally outplaying their opponents in the early stages. However, Torquay had been good value for their win and, as a terrace philosopher once observed, 'Football is a game of two halves!'

In a remarkable phase in the mid-1960s, the West Ham trio of Bobby Moore, Martin Peters and Geoff Hurst appeared for three successive years in showpiece finals at Wembley. They lined up alongside players who would later leave their mark on Devon soccer. The West Ham team that won the 1964 FA Cup contained John Bond and Ken Brown. Both defenders ended their League careers at Torquay and Ken Brown later managed Argyle. The Hammers' two-goal hero of the 1965 European Cup Winner's final was winger Alan Seeley, who moved to Plymouth two years later, where injury ended his playing days. England's finest hour against West Germany in the 1966 World Cup featured the side's youngest player, Alan Ball, who moved into management at Exeter.

EXETER CITY 0 PLYMOUTH ARGYLE 2
FA CUP FIRST ROUND, 17 NOVEMBER 1956
(ATTENDANCE 13,855)

City (2-3-5): George Hunter; Brian Doyle, John Ferrier; Ray John, Keith Harvey, John Porteous; Ed Buckle, Keith Thomas, Arnold Mitchell, Jim Currie, Graham Rees; Manager: Norman Dodgin.
Argyle (2-3-5): Jimmy Gee; George Robertson, Pat Jones; Johnny Williams, Peter Langman, Rex Tilley; Malcolm Davies, Eric Davis, Neil Langman, Peter Kearns, Jack Rowley (player-manager).

The 'deep-lying centre forward', first seen in Britain when Hungary crushed England 6-3 at Wembley in 1953, had been adopted by many League teams, notably Manchester City. Exeter City's answer to Nandor Hidegkuti and Don Revie was defender Arnold Mitchell, who made the tactical switch for this cup-tie against the 'old enemy'. However, it was Argyle who handed out a footballing lesson, and City's attempt to blind Argyle with science failed dismally through their insistence on sticking to 'route one' football. As Exeter displayed the fine art of 'kick and rush', one Grecian supporter was heard to bawl at his team in despair: 'Give it to Plymouth, at least we will see some soccer!'

The Pilgrims had been relegated the previous season to join Exeter and Torquay in Third Division (South) for the first time since 1930. After a shaky

Argyle scorer Neil Langman.

start to the campaign, they were lying bottom of the League, and this cup match was easily their finest display so far. This was no blood and thunder derby, but an Argyle exhibition match which made a mockery of their lowly position. City 'keeper George Hunter was kept busy during the opening exchanges, and had to make his best saves from Argyle's marauding defenders. He dived to stop a fierce drive from wing-half Johnny Williams and then made a world class stop, tipping a blinding shot from centre half Peter Langman over the bar. Peter's brother, Neil, showed how it should be done in the thirty-fourth minute. The Argyle centre

Argyle player-manager Jack Rowley.

forward soared to meet a cross from player-manager Jack Rowley, and buried the ball in the net with a magnificent header.

Plymouth continued to dominate after the break and increased their lead in the sixty-third minute, with a goal from Jack Rowley. The former England player showed all the class that had won him League and FA Cup honours with Manchester United, when he cut in from the left wing and let fly with a drive. Hunter never moved as the ball flew past him into the roof of the net. The shaken 'keeper made his first mistake of the match a minute later when he fumbled another Rowley rocket. Full-back Brian Doyle came to the rescue and cleared the ball, surrounded by furious Plymouth forwards who appealed unsuccessfully to the referee that the ball had crossed the goal line. Hunter redeemed himself on several occasions before the end of the match, as a brilliant display of goalkeeping saved the Grecians from a heavy defeat.

This had been the first FA Cup meeting of the Devon rivals since their Southern League days in 1909. By an amazing coincidence, when the cup draw was made, Argyle's reward for this convincing victory was yet another away derby, setting up their first-ever FA Cup clash with Torquay United.

TORQUAY 1 PLYMOUTH ARGYLE 0
FA CUP SECOND ROUND, 8 DECEMBER 1956
(ATTENDANCE 15,830)

United (2-3-5): Mervyn Gill; John Smith, Harry Smith; Dennis Lewis, Griff Norman, Norman Lloyd; Ron Shaw, Ronald 'Sam' Collins, Jack Smith, Tony Collins; Manager: Eric Webber.
Argyle (2-3-5): Harry Brown; George Robertson, Pat Jones; Johnny Williams, Peter Langman, Rex Tilley; Neil Dougall, Eric Davis, Neil Langman, Peter Kearns, Jack Rowley (player-manager).

Torquay United's preparations for this cup-tie were seriously disrupted when midfield maestro Don Mills was called away to his native Yorkshire to attend the funeral of his father. 'The Don' is still regarded as the finest player to ever pull on a shirt for United, but an enforced absence gave his colleagues the chance to prove that they were more than 'a one-man team'. Argyle had problems of a different kind. For the first time since their entry to the League in 1920, their ascendancy in Devon soccer was seriously under threat, as their recent form had left them propping up the League.

It was estimated that half of the large crowd were Argyle supporters, and they had plenty to cheer for as the Pilgrims stormed into the attack from the start.

Left: *Jack Smith takes over the role of midfield general.* Right: *Sam Collins hits the winner.*

Plymouth enjoyed early territorial advantage, and wing-half Johnny Williams tested 'keeper Mervyn Gill with a full-blooded drive from long range. Argyle squandered a great opportunity to go in front, when player-manager Jack Rowley tore into the box and rounded the 'keeper. With only full-back John Smith covering the line, the winger carefully teed up the ball and let fly with a tremendous shot – which, to the delight of United fans, screamed wide of the target.

Argyle were made to pay for this let-off just before half-time, when a penalty was awarded against George Robertson. A minute earlier, the full-back had crashed into former Plymouth forward Harold Dobbie, and was fortunate that the referee turned down United appeals for a foul. It was asking for trouble when his next tackle brought down Jack Smith in the box. Top scorer Sam Collins took the spot-kick, and Harry Brown had no chance of preventing United from walking off to the dressing room with a thoroughly undeserved lead.

The second half belonged to Torquay, as Plymouth seemed to have played themselves out in the Plainmoor mud. Having soaked up so much pressure in the first period, United's defence were now well on top and gave the Argyle attack few opportunities to bring their side back into the match. Don Mills' replacement, former Liverpool player, Jack Smith, began to have more influence in midfield. Former Plymouth forward Harold Dobbie roved tirelessly from flank to flank, and Ron Shaw showed why Plainmoor fans had dubbed him the 'wing wizard'. Man of the Match was wing-half Norman Lloyd, who dropped back alongside centre-back Griff Norman to snuff out the double spearhead of Neil Langman and Eric Davies. After a torrid start to the game, the Torquay team had rallied to confound the doom and gloom merchants among their own terrace critics, who had prophesied a heavy defeat for a team taking the field without star man Don Mills.

In August 1983, Torquay United footballer Roy Carter dashed to Plainmoor to play in a pre-season friendly against Plymouth Argyle, only hours after delivering a baby in a family drama which started in the early hours of Saturday morning. Roy's wife went into labour at their home in St German's, Cornwall, and the couple's second child, a healthy baby boy, arrived so fast that there was no time to reach the hospital. Ironically, Roy's wife, Wendy, had earlier spent five months in hospital during a difficult pregnancy. The proud father told the 'Herald Express': 'It was me or nobody, so I had to deliver the baby myself. One minute Wendy was in labour and the next I was standing there with the baby in my arms. Wendy was terrific. She told me what to do most of the time. A couple of neighbours came round after hearing what was going on, and one of them used to be a nurse, so that was a great help. It was a fantastic experience.' The midfield player spent a year at Torquay and, following spells with Bristol Rovers and Newport County, moved back to Devon in 1987 to end his League career with Exeter City.

PLYMOUTH ARGYLE 2 TORQUAY UNITED 1
FOOTBALL LEAGUE CUP, SECOND ROUND (REPLAY), 7 NOVEMBER 1960
(ATTENDANCE 7,982)

Argyle (2-3-5): Geoff Barnsley; Reg Wyatt, Bryce Fulton; John 'Cardiff' Williams, Gordon Fincham, George Robertson; Peter Anderson, Johnny Williams, George Kirby, Wilf Carter, Ken Maloy; Joint Managers: Neil Dougall and George Taylor.
United (2-3-5): Mervyn Gill; Colin Bettany, Jimmy James; Dave Hancock, Alan Smith, Colin Rawson; Larry Baxter, Geoff Cox, Tommy Northcott, Don Mills, Ernie Pym; Manager: Eric Webber.

The Football League Cup was launched in 1960. Adding to an already congested fixture list, the knock-out competition did not meet with wholehearted enthusiasm and five top clubs boycotted the tournament. The lop-sided draw gave Torquay a bye into the second round where they were drawn at home to meet Plymouth, who had progressed to this stage by eliminating Southport. A waterlogged Plainmoor pitch forced a postponement and, much to the disgust of United fans, a decision was taken to switch the tie to Home Park. Following a 1-1 draw, with goals from United's Don Mills and Argyle's Wilf Carter, the replay controversially gave Plymouth home advantage once again.

Torquay returned to Home Park with optimism, having notched up a sequence of thirteen unbeaten matches since their promotion to the Third Division. Since the draw with United, the Pilgrims had suffered a heavy defeat at home to Liverpool and their League form seemed to justify the critics' tag of 'too good for the Third Division, not good enough for the Second'.

In an age when substitutes were not allowed, Torquay's chances received a severe setback when Don Mills, Colin Bettany and Tom Northcott all picked up injuries in the first half. The visitors faced an uphill struggle to stay in the tie, but the match started off promisingly when they won a corner and inside-forward Geoff Cox fired in a shot, which took a slight deflection off defender Gordon Fincham, before beating 'keeper Geoff Barnsley. The Pilgrims' prolific marksman, Wilf Carter, hit a tremendous drive against the underside of the bar before the home side equalised after forty minutes. Mervyn Gill dived to tip away a thunderbolt from George Kirby, but was powerless to prevent winger Ken Maloy from following up to ram home the rebound. Torquay were fortunate to leave the field all-square at the interval,

Argyle skipper Johnny Williams' goal settles the tie.

when another Kirby rocket struck the foot of the post. Moments later, the centre forward was thwarted again, when full-back Jimmy James cleared a goal-bound header off the line. Argyle confirmed their superiority after the break, and the best goal of the night came from skipper Johnny Williams. Switched from wing-half to inside forward for this match, he collected the ball on the edge of the area and struck the winner through a ruck of players into the corner of the net.

Plymouth's run in the new competition ended after three titanic battles with Aston Villa in the fourth round. A thrilling 3-3 battle at Villa Park was followed by a goal-less home draw in a match abandoned after ninety minutes. The second replay at Home Park resulted in a pulsating 5-3 victory for the Midland giants, who went on to become the first holders of the trophy when they defeated Rotherham United in a two-leg final.

United's inspirational Don Mills was injured early on.

Generations of Devon football fans have experienced many days when the highlight of the match has come as they tucked into their favourite half-time treat and swilled it down with a scalding hot cup of tea! After a gruelling ten-year wait for success, Argyle supporters presented skipper Freddie Titmus with a giant pasty, carried out with due ceremony on a stretcher before the last home game of the 1929/30 promotion season. The Pilgrims have often utilized pasties as lucky mascots and, before their FA Cup defeat at Chelsea in January 1936, supporters paraded a pasty adorned in green and white ribbons through the streets of London. At Plainmoor in January 1992, Gulls reserve Chris Curran was tucking into a pasty when he was called up to replace injured Matt Elliot, twenty minutes before the kick-off against Exeter. Playing on a full stomach obviously did him no harm, as the defender starred in United's victory and received the Man of the Match award. Considering the importance of pasties in local soccer, it's surprising that no Devon club has run out wearing shirts sponsored by an enterprising baker – which reminds me of the the Grecian wag who, upon hearing that Ivor Doble had become chairman of the club, commented drolly, 'Pity it's not Ivor Dewney, at least we'd get a decent pasty at The Park!'

EXETER CITY 0 TORQUAY UNITED 3
FOOTBALL LEAGUE CUP, FIRST ROUND (REPLAY), 28 AUGUST 1967
(ATTENDANCE 5,700)

City (4-2-4): John Smout; Cecil Smyth, Ernie Wilkinson, Mike Balson, Campbell Crawford; Jim Blain, Cliff Huxford; Stuart Hart, Bruce Stuckey, Mickey Fudge, Keith Whatling; Manager; Frank Broome.
United (4-2-4): John Dunn; Eric Burgess, John Bond, Ken Brown, Bobby Baxter; Doug Clarke Jimmy Dunne; Ronnie Barnes, Jim Fryatt, Robin Stubbs, John Docker; Manager: Frank O'Farrell.

Having gained a goal-less draw at Plainmoor, Exeter City were in confident mood for this first round replay, but crashed out of the competition to a Torquay side which recorded their fourth match in a row without conceding a goal. The Gulls were riding high in the Third Division, and gave a much-improved display in the return at St James Park to impose their superiority over their spirited the Fourth Division neighbours. The architect of United's victory was two-goal John Docker. The on-loan striker from Coventry added punch to the attack and gave a supreme illustration of opportunism, which proved to be the difference between the two sides.

Both teams had injury problems before the match, which were exacerbated by some crunching tackles in this keenly-fought derby. It was surprising that all the players finished the match without either being stretchered off or sent off the field by an extremely tolerant referee. Midway through the first half, United

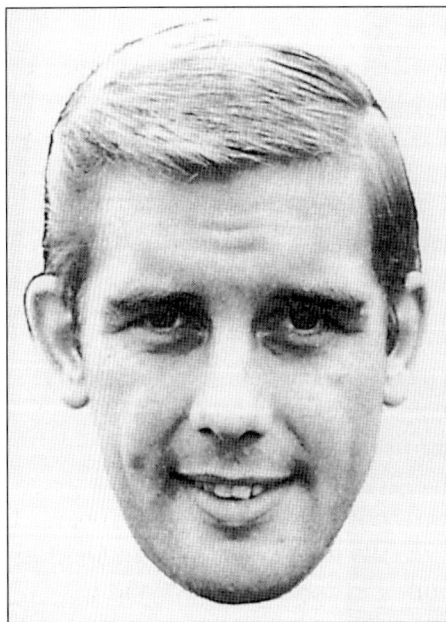

United's John Dunn preserves his unbeaten record.

Torquay United, 1967/68 season. Second row, far right (seated): John Docker.

took the lead when City centre half Ernie Wilkinson headed out a clearance to the wing, where John Docker latched onto the ball and fired in a 20-yard shot which streaked past 'keeper John Smout.

The Gulls held the advantage until the break, and then faced a City side that came out fighting for the second half. It took some fine saves by John Dunn to keep his impressive unbeaten record intact. The 'keeper also had luck on his side when former United player Bruce Stuckey cleverly put through Mickey Fudge, whose fierce low drive thudded against the upright. Immediately, City paid for this miss when United added a second in the seventieth minute. Striker Robin Stubbs collected a pass wide on the right and crossed the ball into the middle, where Docker controlled the ball and hit it into the net in one glorious movement.

This setback failed to quell the Grecians' resolve, and the home fans gasped as Bruce Stuckey failed by inches to steer in a Keith Watling cross. Many of City's promising and adventurous attacks floundered in the face of the calm defensive qualities of former West Ham veterans Ken Brown and John Bond. This League Cup derby must have seemed a world away from their recent taste of success with the Hammers in FA Cup and European Cup Winners competition, yet their calm authority was a decisive factor as United battled to keep City at bay.

Almost on full-time, Exeter's resistance was finally broken when they gifted United a third goal. Striker Jim Fryatt lashed in a shot which John Smout appeared to have covered. As he went down to collect the ball, the 'keeper momentarily lost concentration and, to his horror, the ball slipped through his grasp and trickled over the line.

EXETER CITY 1 PLYMOUTH ARGYLE 0
FOOTBALL LEAGUE CUP, FIRST ROUND, (2ND REPLAY), 26 AUGUST 1968
(ATTENDANCE 10,884)

City (4-2-4): Peter Shearing; Cecil Smyth, John Newman, Keith Harvey, Mike Balson; John Kirkham, Jim Blain; John Mitten, Alan Banks, Pete Bullock (sub: Dermot Curtis), David Pleat; Manager: Frank Broome.
Argyle (4-3-3): Pat Dunne; Mike Reeves, Duncan Neale, Bobby Saxton, Colin Sullivan; Norman Piper, John Hore, Dave Burnside; Steve Davey (sub: John Tedesco), Mike Bickle, Richard Reynolds; Manager: Billy Bingham.

'All we are saying is give us a goal,' sang the long-suffering supporters of both teams, as they endured this turgid second replay. A total of 32,000 people watched the three matches, and it took 328 minutes of this marathon League Cup tie to finally produce a last-gasp goal with only two minutes of extra time remaining. Exeter had initially had the best of a scoreless draw at Home Park, but had been unable to make use of home advantage in the replay, which also ended in stalemate after extra time. Third Division Argyle appeared to have weathered the worst that their opponents could throw at them, and were favourites to finally kill off their rivals in this third encounter on neutral territory at Plainmoor. City, however, parading four former Pilgrims, John Newman, Peter Shearing, Alan Banks and John Mitten, defied their lowly position in the Fourth Division to emerge as serial giant-killers in this derby war of attrition.

Shot-shy forwards continued to astonish the spectators with their ineptitude in front of goal. In the opening exchanges, John Kirkham wasted a golden opportunity to open the scoring, when he mishit a shot after Dave Pleat and Jim Blain had provided the opening. Before Argyle's defence could recover, Peter Bullock and Kirkham, again, both totally miskicked to squander another chance. Argyle's best effort before the break was a Mike Bickle drive, which passed harmlessly across the face of the goal. In the second half, Argyle began to get their range and, after a cross from Steve Davey had bounced off the bar, 'keeper Peter Shearing held a low 'banana' shot from Norman Piper. Bobby Saxton headed wide and Dave Burnside, Richard Reynolds and Mike Bickle all missed good chances. With twenty minutes to go, Argyle substitute John Tedesco came on and immediately entered the fray by blazing over the bar to ironic cheers from the crowd. A despairing cry from an Exeter supporter summed up the feelings of the crowd as the saga entered extra-time: 'Come on score ... anybody!'

As this point, City brought on their substitute, Dermot Curtis. The Eire international brought much needed urgency to the Grecians' attack, and created the chance which prevented a third replay and put both sets of fans out of their misery. He slid a through ball to John Kirkham, who atoned for his earlier lapses by crashing the ball past Pat Dunne. To the relief of everyone concerned, the

Exeter City, 1968/69 season. Back row, third from left: John Kirkham.

tie was over. The long wait proved worthwhile for Exeter, who were amply rewarded for their efforts with a second round clash against Sheffield Wednesday. The Owls were soundly beaten in a giant-killing act at St James Park, before City were eliminated in another highly profitable plum draw against Tottenham Hotspur at White Hart Lane.

Arsenal emerged as the world's most glamorous soccer club under manager Herbert Chapman in the Depression-hit 1930s. The League Championship went to Highbury four seasons out of five between 1931-1935, flanked by FA Cup victories in 1930 and 1936. Chapman splashed out extravagant fees to secure the services of the players he wanted. This included the first £10,000 transfer for former Plymouth Argyle inside forward David Jack in 1928. The Gunners' boss regarded his signings as bargain buys, and this was certainly so in the case of the £2,000 paid for Exeter City's sixteen-year-old winger, Cliff 'Boy' Bastin, in 1929. A few months before his sudden death in January 1934, Chapman bought Torquay United winger Ralph Birkett for £1,500 and Plymouth Argyle centre forward Ray Bowden for £5,000.

PLYMOUTH ARGYLE 2 TORQUAY UNITED 2
FOOTBALL LEAGUE CUP, ROUND ONE, 13 AUGUST 1969
(ATTENDANCE 15,199)

Argyle (4-3-3): Pat Dunne; Mike Reeves, George Foster, Fred Molyneaux, Duncan Neale; Norman Piper, John Hore, Dave Burnside; Trevor Shepherd, Richard Reynolds, Aiden Maher (sub: Mike Bickle); Manager: Billy Bingham. United (4-3-3): Andy Donnelly; Kenny Sandercock, John Benson, Bill Kitchener, Brian Faulkes; Jimmy Dunne, Mickey Cave, Tommy Mitchinson; Eric Welsh (sub: Alan Welsh), John Rudge, Fred Binney; Manager Allan Brown.

This League Cup clash was described in the *Herald Express* as 'a masterpiece of excitement and crowd-thrilling entertainment with both sides giving every ounce of energy and enthusiasm'. It was also one of the few period's in the Gulls' history when they had a team capable of matching the Pilgrims, who had been relegated the previous season to join their South Devon rivals in the Third Division. Only a terrific second-half fightback enabled Argyle to take this tie to a replay.

In the opening passage of play, United's small forward line displayed great ball skills and created havoc in the opposition defence. Eric Welsh and John Rudge combined to put Tommy Mitchinson through, and his fierce shot was beaten away by 'keeper Pat Dunne. Further attempts from Mitchinson and Mickey Cave were cleared by an increasingly nervous defence, before Argyle took an undeserved lead against the run of play. Midway through the first half, Norman Piper curled in a cross which Andy Donnelly came out to collect. Defender Bill Kitchener, under pressure from Dave Burnside, intercepted the ball and inadvertently ran it into his own net. Unperturbed, the Gulls hit back with two goals before the break. Ironically, the scorers were two players who might have been on Plymouth's books. Earlier that year, Argyle had declined to sign Northern Ireland international Eric Welsh when he had been on loan at Home Park, while Plymouth-born striker Fred Binney had slipped through the scouting net and would not join Argyle until much later in his career.

Fred Binney skilfully paved the way for Welsh to stab in the equaliser, then midfield maestro Tommy Mitchinson teased Duncan Neale on the right touchline, before centring for Binney to score. After the interval, Argyle utilised strong-arm tactics to try and force their way back into the match and had three players booked for displays of temperament and bad tackles. Skill was still abundant however, with former Aston Villa player Mitchinson dubbed the 'Prime Minister of Plainmoor', and Argyle's former West Bromwich Albion and England under-23 international Dave Burnside, who levelled the scores in the seventieth minute. Aiden Maher had been substituted by Mike Bickle, who seized on a sloppy United throw-in and powered his way past Bill Kitchener before squaring the ball back to Burnside – who rammed a shot into the corner of the net.

The following week, the replay at Plainmoor was decided in United's favour by a solitary goal scored by John Rudge. Three days later, Argyle returned to Torquay and

Left: *Eric Welsh scores against his former club.* Right: *Fred Binney puts United in the lead.*

exacted revenge in a League fixture, winning by the odd goal in three. Plymouth completed the double in the return at Home Park, when they gave United a six-goal drubbing on Boxing Day!

During the 1926 General Strike, a most unusual soccer match took place at Home Park, when Police played Strikers in a public relations exercise. The Strikers won 2-1, while, in the centre of Plymouth, uniformed officers were attempting to quell a riot caused when the local tram service started to run, manned by strike-breakers! In May 1914, Exeter City undertook a 'fly the flag' tour of South America. They played five matches in Argentina and three in Brazil. The trip was full of incident, particularly when City scored against Racing Club, the Argentine League champions, and the home team secretary drew a gun and threatened to shoot the referee! On another occasion, several City players were arrested on charges of indecent exposure, for removing their shirts on a beach in Rio de Janeiro. By the time the players had made the arduous sea journey back to England, the First World War had broken out. In 1937, the German battle-ship Schlesian *made an official visit to Torquay, and a team of crewmen played against United in a testimonial match for full-back Lew Tapp. As the German band struck up their national anthem, the sailors stunned the Plainmoor crowd by giving the Nazi salute. Two years later, the ship took part in the bombardment of Poland!*

TORQUAY UNITED 0 PLYMOUTH ARGYLE 2
FOOTBALL LEAGUE CUP, FIRST ROUND, 29 AUGUST 1973
(ATTENDANCE 6,996)

United (4-3-3): Mike Mahoney; Ian Twitchin, Clint Boulton, Dave Stocks, Phil Sandercock; Ken Sandercock, Mal Lucas (sub: Cliff Jackson), Cliff Myers; Steve Morrall, John Rowles, Bruce Stuckey; Manager: Malcolm Musgrove.
Argyle (4-2-4): Jim Furnell; Mike Dowling, Bobby Saxton, Dave Provan, Colin Sullivan; John Hore, Ernie Machin; Brian Johnson (sub: Hugh Reed), Steve Davey, Jimmy Hinch, Harry Burrows; Manager: Tony Waiters.

In a dour and drab derby League Cup-tie on a late summer's evening at Plainmoor, there was little evidence to suggest that Argyle were taking a tentative step towards a wonderful cup run which would lead to the latter stages of the competition. Miraculously, by the New Year, their supporters were beginning to believe a prediction in the 1974 edition of *Old Moore's Almanac* that a team wearing green and black would appear at Wembley!

The first half was a colourless affair, which degenerated into a niggling midfield battle, enlivened only by the occasional flashes of brilliance from Gulls' winger Bruce Stuckey. The home side had the earliest clear-cut scoring opportunity, when full-back Phil Sandercock placed a free-kick perfectly at the feet of his older brother, Ken, who was standing unmarked in front of goal. The chance went begging as he scooped the ball high over the bar. After this incident, United were disappointing up front and Argyle 'keeper Jim Furnell was rarely troubled for the remainder of the match.

Mike Mahoney made impressive saves.

Two goals for Argyle's Steve Davey.

After the interval, Furnell's counterpart, Mike Mahoney, was called upon to make several impressive saves, as Plymouth upped the tempo in an effort to break the deadlock. The tie sparked into life in the fifty-third minute when Steve Davey showed ruthless efficiency with a beautifully taken goal. A series of mishaps in the United defence created the chance. Mal Lucas lost possession to John Hore, whose shot cannoned off defender Dave Stocks. The ball ran to Davey on the opposite side of the area, and his measured shot flew past Mahoney. The United defence circled the wagons, as Argyle surrounded the goalmouth. A low drive from Ernie Machin shaved the base of the upright and Mahoney brought off a tremendous save from winger Harry Burrows. The striking power of Steve Davey extended Argyle's lead in the seventieth minute, when he swivelled on a defence-splitting pass from centre forward Jim Hinch and smashed in a shot from 20 yards. From that moment, the result was never beyond doubt and only Mahoney's heroics denied substitute Hugh Reed and prevented Davey from collecting a hat-trick.

Fans with long memories may well have written off this game as one of the least interesting meetings between the old rivals, but the result took on renewed significance as the Pilgrims made spectacular progress through the following rounds. They eliminated Portsmouth, Burnley, Queens Park Rangers and Birmingham before Old Moore's prophecy and the Third Division side's Wembley dream were cruelly shattered in a close-fought two-leg semi-final against Manchester City. Ironically, when Argyle had battled through to the same stage of the competition in 1965, prominent amongst their ranks was Blues manager, Tony Book!

EXETER CITY 2 PLYMOUTH ARGYLE 2
FOOTBALL LEAGUE CUP, FIRST ROUND, 13 AUGUST 1977
(ATTENDANCE 6,712)

City (4-3-3): John Baugh; John Templeman, Bobby Saxton, Peter Hatch, John Hore; Graham Weeks, Lammie Robertson, Nicky Jennings; Bobby Hodge, Tony Kellow, Alan Beer; sub: Keith Bowker; Manager: Bobby Saxton.
Argyle (3-5-2): Paul Barron; Kevin Smart, George Foster, John Uzzell; Brian Johnson, Mick Horswill, John Delve, John Craven, Alan Rogers; Terry Austin, Mike Trusson; sub: Dave Sutton; Manager: Mike Kelly.

On the eve of this cup-tie, Exeter City midfielder, Lammie Robertson, learned that his proposed transfer to Norwich City had collapsed. Overcoming the disappointment of losing a chance to play in the top flight, he put on an amazing show of penalty taking, and might have had a hat-trick but for the intervention of the referee. The official's correct interpretation of the rules sparked outrage amongst mystified supporters, and a mindless minority of hooligans soured a great game by resorting to an emerging pattern of violence which marred many derby matches.

City took an early lead when Lammie Robertson was fouled in the area by Argyle skipper, John Craven. Robertson hit the ball past the despairing left-hand dive of 'keeper Paul Barron, but was ordered to retake the penalty as the ball was not placed correctly on the spot. This time, Lammie sent the 'keeper the wrong way, as he placed the ball into the opposite corner of the net. The home side came close to extending their lead when a thundering drive from John Templeman shook the crossbar. The Pilgrims hit back just before half time, when striker Mike Trusson struck twice in three minutes to give Argyle the lead. The first came from a Brian Johnson cross which was headed powerfully past 'keeper John Baugh. The second followed a Craven free-kick, which was flicked on by Terry Austin for Trusson to crash into the net.

Ten minutes after the interval, Tony Kellow appeared to have snatched the equaliser, but the whistle had already blown for a foul committed by Paul Barron, who was clinging onto the striker's boot as the ball went over the line during a goalmouth scramble. Lammie Robertson stepped up once again and nonchalantly levelled the scores. Drama struck midway through the second half when Exeter were awarded a third penalty, after skipper John Craven pushed Alan Beer whilst attempting to clear a cross. This time, Paul Barron anticipated Robertson's intentions and dived to palm the ball away, but Lammie followed up quickly and blasted the ball past the prostrate 'keeper. Controversy ensued when the goal was disallowed, as two City players were adjudged to have encroached in the area. The referee, Les Burdon, refused Exeter appeals to let the kick be retaken and awarded an indirect free-kick to Plymouth.

The game ended in uproar, but the man in charge politely pointed out to waiting newsmen, that the laws clearly state if an attacking player encroaches and a penalty rebounds into play, then an indirect kick shall be awarded to the defending team.

Penalty specialist Lammie Robertson.

So-called 'fans' with no respect for laws of any kind went on the rampage. Fencing was torn down at St James Park, and running battles in the town centre resulted in damage to shops. The second leg resulted in a scoreless draw, before Exeter went through to the second round, with the only goal of the game scored by Alan Beer in a replay at Home Park.

Before referees declared open season on goalkeepers in the 1990s, it was a rare event to see one sent off. In December 1952, Bristol City were awarded a penalty at home to Exeter City, and Northern Ireland international goalkeeper Hugh Kelly was booked for throwing mud at the ball, in disgust at the referee's decision. He then went back between the posts and saved the spot-kick, but continued to protest and talked himself into an early bath! Forward Jimmy Dailey took over in goal, but ten-man City lost 4-1. Torquay United's Eire international Bill Hayes had the misfortune to break his leg, when he collided heavily with an oncoming forward at Swindon in March 1954. To add insult to injury, the referee awarded a penalty against him, as he was stretchered unconscious from the field. Full-back Jimmy Drinkwater went in goal and saved the spot-kick, but could not prevent a 6-1 defeat. Plymouth Argyle player-manager Peter Shilton had enjoyed a twenty-five-year career at the top, winning 125 caps for England and appearing in over 1,000 League and cup games, before he earned the wrath of officials in the crackdown on the 'professional foul'. He was sent off at Hull, after bringing down a forward in August 1992. Defender Nicky Marker donned the 'keeper's jersey and produced a brilliant double-save from the penalty then the follow-up, and was not to blame for the goals in the 2-0 defeat!

TORQUAY UNITED 3 EXETER CITY 2
FOOTBALL LEAGUE TROPHY, GROUP MATCH, 21 AUGUST 1982
(ATTENDANCE 2,384)

United (4-3-3): Graham Horn; John Doyle, Clive Wiggington Brian Wilson, Bruce Rioch (player-manager); Steve Grapes, Graham Jones, Frank Sheridan; Jackie Gallagher, Steve Cooper, Ray Bishop.
City: (4-3-3): Len Bond; Graham Kirkup, Stan McEwan, Frank Howarth, Keith Viney; Martin Rogers, John Delve, Dave Harle; Peter Rogers, Tony Kellow, Dave Pullar (sub: Ray Pratt); Manager: Brian Godfrey.

The Football League Trophy was introduced in 1981 for clubs from the Third and Fourth Divisions. It was the first tournament to give players from the lower reaches of the League a realistic chance of reaching a Wembley final. The competition developed into the Associate Members Cup and became better known by a variety of sponsors names, including Freight Rover Trophy, Sherpa Van Trophy and Auto Windscreens Shield. Originally, teams were organized into groups of four, with the winner going forward to the knock-out stage of the competition. In its second year, Exeter and Torquay were drawn in a group with Newport County and Bristol City. Before this final group match, when the derby rivals kicked-off in the evening, Newport had already secured their passage to the quarter-finals with a big win earlier in the day against Bristol City. With nothing more than a runners-up spot at stake, United and City could have been forgiven for coasting through a meaningless match, but they served up a magnificent feast of soccer for the loyal band of supporters who turned out at Plainmoor.

The Gulls nearly got the match off to a spectacular start, when Ray Bishop

Torquay United team. Front row, third from right: Brian Wilson.

outpaced the defence and drove against the post with a rasping shot in the opening minute. City hit back and took the lead in the seventeenth minute when winger Dave Pullar chipped in a pass from Stan McEwan. Tony Kellow almost made it two with a spectacular volley, which sped inches wide of the target, before United leader Steve Cooper equalised with a splendid header from a Steve Grapes corner. Torquay were in the ascendancy, and Ray Bishop rounded off a good run by bouncing a 35-yard shot off the cross bar, and Len Bond saved well from a Frank Sheridan header.

The Gulls took the lead early in the second half. Graham Jones popped up on the left flank and coolly crossed with the outside of his right foot for Steve Cooper to nod in another delightful header. The fearless centre forward was later denied a cracking hat-trick effort for offside. City's Ray Pratt, a half-time substitute for Dave Pullar, levelled the scores, tapping in from close range when 'keeper Graham Horn brilliantly pushed out a rising drive from Peter Rogers. A draw seemed on the cards until United trialist Jackie Gallagher earned himself a contract when he made the winner ten minutes from the end. The former Lincoln and Peterborough striker determinedly broke through a challenge on the right byline and squared the ball back for defender Brian Wilson to hammer home from the edge of the six-yard box. With the opening matches of the League season only a week away, team managers Bruce Rioch and Brian Godfrey could feel well pleased with their respective teams' performances in this cup match, which ended up serving as a useful pre-season friendly.

An international incident occurred before a match in the 1930s, when the England team were coerced into giving the Nazi salute by FA secretary, and former Exeter City reserve goalkeeper, Stanley Rous. He was acting under orders from the British government, who did not wish to insult the host country, despite the fact they were preparing to wage war in Europe. Lining up for England were three of the finest players ever associated with Devon clubs. Exeter-born winger Cliff Bastin had played for his home club before becoming a legend at Arsenal; Charlton skipper Don Welsh was making his international debut, and had been discovered by Torquay United and Aston Villa's Frank Broome would later have two spells as manager at St James Park. The propaganda machine of Hitler's 'Master Race', forecast an emphatic victory over England, but the home side were humiliated 6-3 in front of over 100,000 spectators. The following day, Frank Broome turned out for Villa, who refused to give the Nazi salute, before they beat a German Select XI. Scottish international, and future Torquay United manager, Alex Massie, led the players' protest. When Stanley Rous implored the team to comply with the wishes of the German officials, he was told: 'Tell 'em to get stuffed!'

PLYMOUTH ARGYLE 2 EXETER CITY 0
FA CUP FIRST ROUND, 20 NOVEMBER 1982
(ATTENDANCE 10,202)

Argyle (4-3-3): Geoff Crudgington; Gordon Nisbett, Chris Harrison, Lindsay Smith, Mike McCartney; Mark Rowe, Kevin Hodges, Leigh Cooper; Jeff Cook, John Sims, Andy Rogers; Manager: Bobby Moncur.
City (4-3-3): Len Bond; Martin Rogers, Nicky Marker, Stan McEwan, Keith Viney; David Harle, John Delve, David Pullar; Steve Neville, Peter Rogers, Tony Kellow; Manager: Brian Godfrey.

Five-figure gates had become something of a rarity at Home Park, but this cup derby against their Third Division rivals drew the highest attendance of the first round. A dour first half, riddled with foul-play, left many supporters wondering whether it had been worth the effort turning up, while a mindless minority amused themselves by hurling missiles into the crowd. The game finally lived up to its pre-match billing when 'Gyles striker John Sims produced a virtuoso performance against his former club to power the Greens along the Wembley trail.

Exeter rarely allowed Argyle to settle into their stride before the interval, and always looked the most likely team to break the deadlock. Steve Neville burst

Kevin Hodges opens the scoring.

through from the halfway line, but was forced out wide to shoot from a narrow angle. Peter Rogers squandered the best opportunity after thirty-two minutes, when he was put through by a clever reverse pass from John Delve. Goalkeeper Geoff Crudgington was drawn out and skilfully rounded by the City forward, who then somehow contrived to miss an unguarded target. Exeter custodian Kevin Bond was rarely troubled and dealt capably with two long-range shots from Kevin Hodges at either end of the first half.

The game was transformed ten minutes after the break, when Jeff Cook hit a stunning shot. John Sims cunningly stepped over an Andy Rogers cross and let it run to Cook, who let fly from 20 yards. It looked a certain goal, but Len Bond brilliantly tipped the ball onto the underside of the bar. A buzz went around the ground, as the Argyle fans realised that the home attack had finally clicked into gear. Five minutes later, Sims tormented the City defence by holding the ball up in the box, before swivelling and crossing to the far post where Kevin Hodges stole in to squeeze the ball home. The Grecians rallied desperately in an effort to level the scores. Tony Kellow just failed to convert a Peter Rogers cross, Martin Rogers cleverly cut inside the box before firing wide, Dave Pullar lashed a drive over the bar, and Steve Neville was also well off target from a good position.

Exeter may have produced the better openings, but Plymouth's ruthlessness in front of goal was the difference between the two sides. Ten minutes from the end, John Sims sealed a memorable match when he ghosted through the City defence and put the result beyond doubt from close range. Running onto a cross from Mike McCartney, he clinically tucked the ball into the corner of the net. Argyle went on to beat Bristol Rovers in the second round, before losing to Watford. A further clash with the Hornets occurred the following season with a memorable FA Cup semi-final at Villa Park, which ended Plymouth's Wembley hopes.

EXETER CITY 5 TORQUAY UNITED 0
AUTOGLASS TROPHY, PRELIMINARY ROUND, 8 DECEMBER 1992,
(ATTENDANCE 2,118)

City (4-3-3): Kevin Miller; Steve Hiley, Scott Daniels, Peter Whiston, Andy Cook; Danny Bailey, Eamonn Collins, Tony Kelly (sub: Toby Redwood); John Hodge, Steve Moran, Eamonn Dolan; Manager: Alan Ball.
United (4-4-2): Jurgen Sommer; Dudley Lewis, Darren Moore, Ian Johnson, Chris Curran (sub: Sean Joyce); Scott Colcombe (sub: Duane Darby), Kevin Hodges, Chris Myers, Paul Trollope; John Fashanu, Adrian Foster; Manager: Ivan Golac.

Hot-shot Steve Moran was the Grecians' hat-trick hero, as he hit a perfect trio of goals. The former Southampton and England Under 21 international scored with a header and both feet in, what was described in a *Western Morning News* headline, as a 'pre-Christmas turkey shoot derby'. The turkeys in question were a Torquay side, who were well and truly stuffed on a mud heap of a pitch at St James Park. The Gulls were a pale imitation of the club that had fought its way to the Wembley final of this competition in 1988, and their travelling fans let them know it with second-half chants of 'What a load of rubbish'.

The result could have been so different, if only United had taken full advantage of the earliest chances of the match. In the opening exchanges, John Fashanu and Adrian Foster both squandered great opportunities by shooting straight at 'keeper Kevin Miller. The rot set in soon after Exeter's opening goal. John Hodge was in sparkling form, and gave Chris Curran a torrid time on the right flank. It was the winger's near-post cross that was converted with a lunging header by Steve Moran after nineteen minutes. Ten minutes before half time, Curran put his goalkeeper under pressure with a risky back-pass. Jurgen Sommers cleared the ball only as far as Eamonn Collins, and the wily midfielder cleverly chipped into an open net from 35 yards.

At the interval, Chris Curran was replaced by Sean Joyce, who played in midfield with Paul Trollope switching to full-back to try and deal with the elusive Hodge. Within five minutes, Trollope had upended the winger in the box and Steve Moran drilled in the penalty with a rasping shot which gave Sommers no chance. In the seventy-fourth minute, John Hodge created another goalscoring opportunity, hitting a low cross which was swept into the net from the edge of the six-yard box by Eamonn Dolan. A woeful Gulls performance was capped five minutes from time when Steve Moran gleefully completed his hat-trick. He finished the rout with a classy shot on the turn at the near post, from a Scott Hiley cross.

Exeter manager Alan Ball was delighted that his players had taken full advantage of United's shortcomings, whilst his opposite number, Paul Compton, was not amused by his team's hapless display. He ordered the United players to report at Plainmoor for training at 8 a.m. the next morning. They were kept at the

The perfect striker's hat-trick for Steve Moran.

ground until 5 p.m., in order to give them a taste of what it is like to do a 'proper job'. After a gruelling training session, many of the culprits found themselves putting in some overtime that night – turning out for the reserves!

War was declared in September 1939, shortly after the football season had started. Exeter City had drawn with Torquay United in the opening League match, but closed down for the duration, when the Football League suspended fixtures. Using players who were waiting for their call-up for military duty, local amateurs and guests from other clubs, United and Argyle continued for one more season in a rearranged South Western Regional Competition with Bristol City, Bristol Rovers, Newport, Swindon, Swansea and Cardiff. The clubs met four times each, and Plymouth emerged as champions, with Torquay runners-up. After the war ended in 1945, all three Devon clubs regrouped for the interim season, before League soccer returned to normality. Plymouth finished bottom of the South League, made up of First and Second Division clubs, while Torquay also finished last in the Third Division (South), with Exeter two places above their local rivals.

Tommy Veale from Dartmouth was awarded the Victoria Cross in 1916, for carrying a wounded officer to safety through heavy fire during the Battle of the Somme. After the war, he served for many years as vice-president of the Plymouth Argyle supporters' club. Exeter City forward Charlie Vowles, who scored in the club's first game in the Football League in 1920, had previously served in India with the 21st Lancers, and taken part in the last cavalry charge made by the British Army. Fighter pilot Dave Mercer was awarded the Distinguished Flying Cross during the Second World War, before becoming a 'flying winger' with Torquay United!

PLYMOUTH ARGYLE 4 EXETER CITY 1
FA CUP SECOND ROUND, 6 DECEMBER 1996
(ATTENDANCE 12,911)

Argyle (5-3-2): Bruce Grobellar; Chris Billy, Tony James, Mick Heathcote, Paul Wotton, Paul Williams; Martin Barlow, Ronnie Mauge, Chris Leadbitter; Mickey Evans, Adrian Littlejohn; Manager: Neil Warnock.
City (3-5-2):Ashley Bayes; Jon Richardson, Noel Blake, Matthew Hare; Mark Chamberlain (sub: Barry McConnell), Marcus Dailly, Chris Myers, Danny Bailey, John Sharpe; Darren Rowbotham, (sub: Leon Braithwaite) Steve Flack; Manager: Peter Fox.

'Devon's Cup Final' was how the pre-match hype described this contest between archrivals Plymouth Argyle and Exeter City. During the build-up, the respective team managers, Neil Warnock and Peter Fox, tried to play down the importance of the game, by emphasising that promotion was the over-riding priority, yet neither could have been under any illusions about what the outcome meant to supporters in this eagerly awaited cup clash. Division Three Exeter were the underdogs, having to face an Argyle team still basking in the glory of promotion won in a play-off final at Wembley the previous season.

Sky television cameras were at Home Park to cover the event, and viewers were not disappointed with the quality of this passionate encounter. The Pilgrims set out to dominate play and won six corners in the first twenty minutes. Exeter seemed to have weathered the storm, before two goals in three minutes put Argyle firmly in control of the match after half an hour. Mickey Evans seized onto the ball in the left-hand corner of the penalty box and fired home a superbly placed low drive past 'keeper Ashley Bayes. Before City could recover their composure, Ronnie Mauge ghosted in to glance in a header from a free-knock, floated in by Paul Williams. As the Argyle players' thoughts were turning to a well-deserved cup of tea, City cut the arrears in stoppage time, with a spectacular 25-yard drive from wing-back John Sharpe. It was a strike worthy of his famous brother, Lee, whose career had begun at Torquay United before he moved on to win honours with Manchester United and England.

City's goal was the first they had scored against Plymouth in four FA Cup meetings. They were not to add to their total, as Argyle resumed their grip on the game after the break. After an hour, the Grecians came close to levelling the scores, when Steve Flack headed a corner just over Bruce Grobbelar's bar. The Exeter goal then came under siege, and shots rained in on Ashley Bayes as Argyle turned the screw. The 'keeper pulled off a tremendous save to deny Plymouth skipper Mick Heathcote's point-blank header, after Paul Wotton had flicked on Martin Barlow's cross.

Persistence finally overcame resistance ten minutes from time. City skipper Danny Bailey conceded possession to Ronnie Mauge in midfield, and the ball broke to Chris Billy, who evaded a challenge from John Sharpe, before striding

Argyle scorers Ronnie Mauge (extreme left) and Chris Billy threaten the Exeter goal.

forward and planting a sublime left-foot shot past Bayes. On the stroke of full time, Adrian Littlejohn converted good approach play on the left flank by Mickey Evans. This fourth goal suddenly turned what had been a hard-fought derby into a resounding victory for the Greens.

In the days before grown men disguised as furry animals and parading as mascots were a constant feature on match days, Exeter City provided some light-hearted half-time relief for the home fans. Soon after Peter Shilton took over as manager of archrivals Plymouth Argyle in 1992, the City faithful were treated to the sight of a turkey, clad in green and white and answering to the name of 'Skeets Shilton', being chased around the ground by a hunter wearing red-and-white apparel and carrying a shot-gun. The turkey trot was brought to an end by a pretend bullet fired in front of the Big Bank. Unfortunately, the Football Association did not see the humour in this form of entertainment, and following threats of an inquiry into the treatment of dumb animals at St James Park, 'Skeets' vanished from the scene! Rumours that he ended up on the Home Park boardroom dinner table were unfounded, as Argyle were relegated and there was no Thanksgiving for these Pilgrims!

EXETER CITY 1 TORQUAY UNITED 0
AUTO WINDSCREENS SHIELD, THIRD ROUND, 25 JANUARY 2000
(ATTENDANCE 2,599)

City (4-3-3): Stuart Naylor, Jon Richardson, Jon Gittens, Chris Curran, Shaun Gale; Jason Rees, Chris Holloway, Paul Buckle; Geoff Breslan (sub: Robert Speakman 30 mins, sub: Rob Dewhurst 90 mins), Gary Alexander, Kofi Nyamah; Acting Manager: Noel Blake.

United (5-3-2): Ryan Northmore; Steve Tully, Wayne Thomas, Lee Russell, Jimmy Aggrey, Jon Nichols; Mick O'Brien (sub: Tony Bedeau), Gary Neil, Kevin Hill; Michael Griffiths, O'Neil Donaldson (sub: Jean Pierre Simb); Manager: Wes Saunders.

Exeter City went into this match as a club in crisis. Three months earlier they had sat proudly at the top of Division Three, before an inexplicable loss of form saw them plunge into the relegation zone. The Manager of the Month curse struck Peter Fox, for, after winning the award in October, a fickle section of Grecian fans turned against him and his five-year reign ended sadly in resignation. Assistant Noel Blake was put in charge of the team and took the opportunity to put out an experimental side for this crucial derby, hoping to gain a place

Wes Saunders – unhappy with his team's performance.

in the last eight of the competition. The United manager, Wes Saunders, selected a side that largely consisted of fringe players who had defeated an under-strength Plymouth Argyle at Home Park in the previous round.

United started brightly with no indication of the disappointing performance which was to follow. Kevin Hill had two glorious chances to put the Gulls ahead in the first few minutes. The chances went begging as he blazed a volley over the bar, and then forced a good save from Stuart Naylor. This last effort proved to be the only shot that Torquay landed on target all night. After dominating during the opening twenty minutes of play, United's game completely fell apart. City sub Gary Speakman replaced the injured Gary Breslan after half-an-hour, and four minutes later, shot Exeter into the lead. The Welsh striker pounced on a through-ball from Gary Alexander and shook off the challenge of defenders Jimmy Aggrey and Wayne Thomas, before rounding 'keeper Ryan Northmore and finishing coolly with a left-foot shot from 12 yards. Just before the interval, Speakman missed a clear opportunity to put the Grecians further ahead when he headed wide.

Torquay continued to have most of the possession in the second half, but found difficulty in stringing a couple of passes together. The standard of crosses posed no danger and the final ball all too often found an untroubled Exeter defence, who were more than happy to sit back and play for time. There was little doubt that City deserved their win, but it was the manner of the defeat that caused the 500 Gulls supporters to jeer their team off St James Park at the final whistle. An opportunity to progress further along the Wembley trail had been thrown away. Manager Wes Saunders slammed his side's lacklustre performance and admitted to the press that he had found it necessary to walk out of the dressing room after the match, in order 'to cool down'. Exeter subsequently reached the semi-final, where a two-leg defeat by Bristol City destroyed their Wembley dream.

STATISTICS
Devon Derby Cup Match Results

Season	FA Cup		
1908/09	R2	Torquay 0-1 Exeter	
1928/29	R2	Torquay 0-1 Exeter	
1938/39	R1	Torquay 3-1 Exeter	
1956/57	R1	Exeter 0-2 Plymouth	
1956/57	R2	Torquay 1-0 Plymouth	
1982/83	R1	Plymouth 2-0 Exeter	
1996/97	R2	Plymouth 4-1 Exeter	

Season	Division Three (South) Cup		
1933/34	Final	Exeter 1-0 Torquay	(played at Home Park)
1936/37	R3	Torquay 2-1 Exeter	

Season	Football League Cup		
1960/61	R1	Torquay 1-1 Plymouth	
	Replay	Plymouth 2-1 Torquay	
1966/67	R1	Exeter 2-2 Torquay	
	Replay	Torquay 1-2 Exeter	
1967/68	R1	Torquay 0-0 Exeter	
	Replay	Exeter 3-0 Torquay	
1968/69	R1	Plymouth 0-0 Exeter	
	Replay	Exeter 0-0 Plymouth	
	Second Replay	Exeter 1-0 Plymouth	(played at Plainmoor)
1969/70	R1	Plymouth 2-2 Torquay	
	Replay	Torquay 1-0 Plymouth	
1973/74	R1	Torquay 0-2 Plymouth	
1975/76	R2	Torquay 1-1 Exeter	
	Replay	Exeter 1-2 Torquay	
1976/77	R1	Plymouth 0-1 Exeter	
1977/78	R1	Exeter 2-2 Plymouth	
	Replay	Plymouth 0-0 Exeter	
	Second Replay	Plymouth 0-1 Exeter	
1978/79	R1/1	Plymouth 1-1 Torquay	
	R1/2	Torquay 1-2 Plymouth	(Plymouth win on aggregate)
1984/85	R1/1	Plymouth 1-0 Torquay	
	R1/2	Torquay 0-1 Plymouth	(Plymouth win on aggregate)
1985/86	R1/1	Plymouth 2-1 Exeter	
	R1/2	Exeter 2-0 Plymouth	(Exeter win on aggregate)
1995/96	R1/1	Torquay 0-0 Exeter	
	R1/2	Exeter 1-1 Torquay	(Torquay win on away goals)

Season	Autowindscreens Shield (formerly Football League Trophy, Associate Members Cup, Freight/Rover Trophy, Sherpa Van Trophy, Autoglass Trophy)		
1981/82	R1	Torquay 1-1 Plymouth	
1982/83	Group Match	Torquay 3-2 Exeter	
1983/84	R1	Plymouth 5-1 Torquay	
1985/86	R1	Torquay 1-0 Exeter	
1989/90	Prelim. Round	Exeter 2-0 Torquay	
1991/92	Prelim. Round	Exeter 2-1 Torquay	
1992/93	Prelim. Round	Exeter 5-0 Torquay	
1992/93	R1	Plymouth 1-0 Exeter	
1992/93	R1	Torquay 2-1 Plymouth	
1993/94	R1	Exeter 1-0 Plymouth	
1994/95	R1	Plymouth 1-3 Exeter	
1999/2000	R2	Plymouth 0-1 Torquay	
1999/2000	R3	Exeter 1-0 Torquay	

4

DEVON PROFESSIONAL CHAMPIONSHIP

Victorious Argyle skipper Steve Castle with the Devon Professional Bowl in 1993.

TORQUAY UNITED 1 PLYMOUTH ARGYLE 2
DEVON PROFESSIONAL CHAMPIONSHIP FINAL, 21 MARCH 1923

United (2-3-5): Bernard Gartrell; Harry Rice, Dick Gaskell, George Thompson, Bob Preston, Tom Hookway; Fred Burch, Tom Townsend, Percy Hill, Bill Burley, Jim Congdon; Manager: Crad Evans.
Argyle (2-3-5): Bill Cook; Billy Forbes, Moses Russell; Jimmy Logan, Jack 'Ginger' Hill, Alf Rowe; Andy Wilson, Harry Raymond, Jack Fowler, Bert Batten, Billy Baker; Manager: Robert Jack.

The Devon Professional Championship was launched as a triangular tournament, with a third of the proceeds from each match going to the Devon County Football Association. In only their second season as a professional club, Torquay United were in the Southern League, where they faced the reserve sides of Plymouth Argyle and Exeter City. It was a surprise, therefore, when the non-League underdogs qualified for the final by beating a strong City side with the only goal of the game at St James Park. The game provided another sensation with a sending-off, which was an extremely rare occurrence back then. United centre forward, and former Exeter player, Percy Hill was dismissed for a foul on City 'keeper Harry Fryer. Even the Exeter players appealed against the decision, given for what appeared to be no more than a normal shoulder charge which was, in those days, within the laws of the game.

Plymouth Argyle received a bye and met Torquay in the inaugural final at Plainmoor. The prospect of springing another shock on League opposition whetted the appetite of United fans and, although the attendance was not recorded, the *Torquay Directory* reported: 'It is many a long day since such a large crowd has been seen at Plainmoor'. Torquay began in sparkling fashion, though they lacked composure in front of goal, wasting good opportunities to take an early lead. Their best effort came from right half Thompson, whose long-range shot dipped just over the crossbar. Plymouth weathered the storm and, after twenty minutes, took the lead with a classic counter-attack. Jack Fowler and Harry Raymond combined to send Andy Wilson away down the right wing. The ball was crossed from the byline and left-winger Billy Baker rose to head past 'keeper Bernie Gartrell from close range. Argyle retained the advantage until the interval and, fifteen minutes after the restart, forged further ahead with a strike from centre forward Jack Fowler. The future Welsh international clinically converted a well-worked move on the left flank by Billy Baker and Bert Batten. Torquay fought determinedly to reduce the arrears, and giant Argyle centre half, Jack Hill, had a tremendous battle to quell the menace of his namesake, Percy, in the United attack. Later that year, Argyle sold Jack Hill to Burnley for a record transfer fee of £6,000 and bought Torquay's Bob Preston to replace him.

Torquay gained their just reward when they pulled a goal back ten minutes from time. Argyle 'keeper Bill Cook failed to hold a shot from Percy Hill, which

Left: *Jack Hill.* Right: *Bob Preston.*

ran to Tom Townsend, who was on hand to tap in a simple chance. The game ended in disappointment for the home supporters, as Argyle held out to become the first winners of the championship. More importantly for Torquay, the event served to enhance the popularity of soccer in the town and furthered the club's long-term ambition to join their derby rivals in the Football League.

EXETER CITY 7 TORQUAY UNITED 1
DEVON PROFESSIONAL CHAMPIONSHIP SEMI-FINAL, 11 FEBRUARY 1925

City (2-3-5): Harry Bailey; Bob Pollard, Stan Charlton; Bob Pullan, Ellis Crompton, Albert Potter; Alf Matthews, Harold 'Jazzo' Kirk, Harold Blackmore, John Davis, George Shelton; Manager: Fred Mavin.
United (2-3-5): Bernard Gartrell; Harry Rice, Tom Millard; Frank Brown, Bert Miller, Alf Leslie; Jimmy Kirkpatrick, Tom Bell, Billy Kellock, Billy Pridham, Dick Bolt; Manager: Harry Raymond.

The *Western Morning Mercury* published the teams on the day of the match and announced that Exeter City would be 'trying the experiment of playing Harold Blackmore at centre forward'. The local discovery was not an automatic choice, despite scoring four goals in five League appearances earlier in the season. He matched this tally against Torquay United, scoring four second-half goals as the Southern League side were pulverised in this Devon Championship semi-final at St James Park. In complete contrast to City's up-and-coming striker, Torquay included a forward coming to the end of a long career. Billy Pridham, now over forty, had played in the Torquay Town side which became the first South Devon club to win the Devon Senior Cup in 1911.

Left: *Harry Bailey saved and scored a penalty!* Right: *Harold Blackmore – an experiment!*

Playing with a strong wind at their backs, the visitors more than held their own during the opening period, before their influential inside forward, Tom Bell, became a limping passenger on the left wing. Right-winger Jimmy Kirkpatrick was also injured, and was forced to leave the field for a long spell to receive treatment. Outnumbered and outplayed, United conceded two goals before half-time, scored by flamboyant leading scorer 'Jazzo' Kirk and wing-half Bob Pullan. The Grecians showed no mercy against their depleted opponents after the interval, and Harold Blackmore scored two quick goals with powerful marksmanship. An opportunity to reduce the arrears went begging when United were awarded a penalty. Left-winger Dick Bolt had his spot-kick well saved by the 'keeper. This miss was made all the more galling when City custodian Harry Bailey later showed how it should be done, slotting home his team's fifth goal from the penalty spot.

Harry Bailey's unique feat of saving and scoring a penalty was followed by Harold Blackmore's hat-trick. Five minutes from the end, Torquay grabbed a consolation goal when Bolt hit an upright and Billy Kellock slammed in the rebound. It was left to Harold Blackmore to have the last word, adding his fourth, and his team's seventh, in the final minute. However, the striker's lethal performance didn't win him a place in the line-up for the championship final, as City lost to Argyle by the odd goal in five. However, it was not long before he established himself in the first team and collected an incredible 45 goals in 77 League appearances. Towards the end of the 1926/27 season, Harold played in a benefit match against Bolton Wanderers, for Exeter colleague Bob Pollard. The Trotters were so impressed, they soon paid £2,150 for his services, replacing David Jack when he moved to Arsenal. The new recruit scored a goal in the 1929 FA Cup final and was the club's top scorer for three seasons.

This triangular tournament was contested fifty times between the 1922/23 and 1994/95 seasons. Unsurprisingly, Plymouth Argyle enjoyed the greatest success, winning the competition outright twenty-three occasions. The Pilgrims also hold a record for a record six consecutive victories, achieved between 1928 and 1934. Exeter won the Devon Championship fourteen times, and dominated the competition in the early 1960s, winning four times on the trot between 1961 and 1965. Torquay United, for so long the Cinderella team of Devon soccer, emerged only eight times as champions. Their best run of three consecutive successes was brought to a halt when they shared the championship with Argyle in the last contest before war was declared in 1939. A Torquay & Exeter Combined XI beat Argyle in 1961, and three competitions started in the 1950s did not reach the final stage!

PLYMOUTH ARGYLE 5 TORQUAY UNITED 1
DEVON PROFESSIONAL CHAMPIONSHIP FINAL, 29 APRIL 1931
(ATTENDANCE 7,500)

Argyle (2-3-5): Harry Cann; Harry Roberts, Len Birks; Bill Fellowes, Harry Bland, Alec Hardie; Tommy Grozier, Ray Bowden, Joe Mantle, Jack Leslie, Sammy Black; Manager: Robert Jack.
United (2-3-5): Joe Wright; Jim Wright, Jack Fowler; Arthur 'Ginger' Phoenix, Jack Butler, Bob Smith; Ralph Birkett, Bill Clayson, Jimmy Trotter, Albert Hutchinson, Harry Waller; Manager: Frank Womack.

Torquay United were making only their third appearance in the final and were hoping to win the championship for the first time ever. The Magpies had turned over Exeter City 6-2 in the semi-final at Plainmoor, but found themselves similarly outplayed at Home Park, as the Second Division outfit emphasised the difference in class which had won them promotion the previous season. Argyle's reserve centre forward, Joe Mantle, made the most of a rare first-team chance to notch a hat-trick. The former Burnley forward made only 15 League appearances at Plymouth before moving on to Chester, but was selected for this match alongside up-and-coming England star Ray Bowden. The pair gave the ex-Arsenal stopper, Jack Butler, a torrid time at the heart of United's defence. The Magpies' attack was given little opportunity to shine, even though it included future England winger, Ralph Birkett, who would later team up with Ray Bowden at Arsenal, as well as Jimmy Trotter, who was to end the season with 26 League goals. This was a club record that was to stand for a quarter of a century.

Joe Mantle got his name on the score sheet within five minutes of the kick-off. Crowd idol Sammy Black weaved his magic down the left wing and turned the ball into the path of the striker, who cleverly chipped advancing 'keeper Joe Wright. United fought back, and came close to equalising, when Albert Hutchinson and Bill Clayson had headers which cleared the bar. Centre half Jack Butler sallied upfield to try a long range shot, which was cleverly deflected by a Trotter back-heel to bring a magnificent reflex save out of Argyle 'keeper Harry Cann. Plymouth gradually regained control and following a corner, Sammy Black latched onto a loose ball in the box and fired in a fierce drive to put Argyle two-up. The home side increased their lead further when Joe Mantle chased a long ball down the middle and shrugged off the challenge of two defenders, as he brilliantly lobbed the ball over Joe Wright's head. The Magpies were denied a penalty when the referee waved play on, after full-back Harry Roberts appeared to handle, but the official had no hesitation in awarding a spot-kick when forward Bill Clayson was upended in the box. Argyle 'keeper Harry Cann got his fingertips to Jack Fowler's penalty kick, but could not prevent the United full-back from reducing the deficit just before half time.

In the second half, Ray Bowden wasted no time in putting the home side

Jack Butler (middle row, fifth from left) – the original 'stopper.'

further ahead, when he capitalised on a mis-kick by Fowler to give Wright no chance with a terrific shot from the edge of the area. Midway through the second half, the best move of the match brought the scoring to an end. Midfield maestro Jack Leslie outwitted the opposition with a defence-splitting pass, which put Joe Mantle through to complete a memorable hat-trick.

In 1925, new offside laws were introduced, reducing the number of defenders between the attacker and the goal from three to two. This inevitably led to an increase in the number of goals scored, and Arsenal shored up their defence by rearranging the team line-up. The centre half, instead of enjoying an attacking role in midfield, became a centre-back – the 'stopper'. Jack Butler, the first player to be deployed in this fashion, ended his playing days at Torquay United and became their manager in 1946. Assisting him as trainer, was Welsh international half-back Bob John, who played alongside him in the Arsenal side which lost to Cardiff in the 1927 FA Cup final. It was the first final to be broadcast on radio, but the game is best remembered because of a costly slip by Dan Lewis which took the cup out of England for the only time. The 'keeper had replaced injured Scottish international Bill Harper, who later served Plymouth Argyle loyally over a period of fifty years as player, trainer, groundsman and kit manager!

EXETER CITY 2 PLYMOUTH ARGYLE 3
DEVON PROFESSIONAL CHAMPIONSHIP FINAL, 27 SEPTEMBER 1933
(ATTENDANCE 5,000)

City (2-3-5): Arthur Chesters, Jim Gray, Richard Hughes; Reg 'Nobby' Clarke, Jack Angus, Harold Webb; Arthur Welsby, Stan Risdon, Fred Whitlow, Tom Walters, John Barnes; Manager: Billy McDevitt.
Argyle (2-3-5): Harry Cann; Harry Roberts, Jimmy Rae; Norman Mackay, Harry Bland, George Reed; Jack Demellweek, George Briggs, Jimmy Cookson, Jack Leslie, Sammy Black; Manager: Robert Jack.

Having eliminated Torquay United in the semi-final at Plainmoor, by three goals to one, Plymouth Argyle travelled away from home once again to meet Exeter City in the final, and recorded their ninth championship victory in the twelfth year of the triangular tournament. A weakened City team, starting without 'keeper Arthur Davies and forward 'Happy' Houghton, were far from disgraced in this close-fought contest against opposition from a higher division. Both teams produced high-class entertainment, and the crowd was treated to some brilliant finishing.

Argyle tended to over-elaborate during the opening exchanges, and Exeter's more direct approach reaped dividends after fifteen minutes. The Grecians took the lead when centre forward Fred Whitlow rose to meet a right-wing cross from Arthur Welsby. Goalkeeper Harry Cann stood rooted to the spot as he was beaten by a magnificent header. However, Plymouth were soon on level terms. Striker

Sammy Black.

Argyle skipper Jack Leslie.

Jimmy Cookson hooked the ball over his head into the path of Jack Leslie, who calmly brought it under control, then slipped it into the net past advancing reserve 'keeper, Arthur Chesters. Fred Whitlow continued to menace Argyle. The defence stood still, as the striker beat the offside trap and ran through to hit a powerful shot, which Harry Cann did well to parry from close range. The Grecians took a deserved lead before the break, when a clever move down the left flank resulted in a telling cross. Whitlow reached it first by sprinting between two defenders, and hit a superb volley that rocketed past Cann into the roof of the net.

When the game resumed after the interval, Argyle wasted no time in levelling the scores with a superb solo effort from the idol of Home Park, Sammy Black. The left-winger fastened onto a long clearance from full-back Jimmy Rae, sped down the flank, then cut inside the defence to score a wonderful goal with a shot from an acute angle. His long-time inside partner, Jack Leslie, began to show his class in midfield, as Plymouth went all out for the winner. City, however, were far from finished. In the gathering gloom of early evening, they believed they had equalised when 'Nobby' Clarke shot from the edge of the area. Harry Cann fumbled the ball, then appeared to step behind the goal line to gather it, as the City forwards closed in. After the referee had consulted his linesman, he awarded an indirect kick to Argyle, apparently for an infringement on the 'keeper.

In a grandstand finish to the game, which ended in semi-darkness, Sammy Black took a corner which Jack Leslie headed in brilliantly for his second goal. The Argyle skipper's winner meant that his team had taken the championship for the sixth year in a row.

115

TORQUAY UNITED 3 PLYMOUTH ARGYLE 0
DEVON PROFESSIONAL CHAMPIONSHIP FINAL, 3 OCTOBER 1934
(ATTENDANCE 5,000)

United (2-3-5): Percy Maggs; Willis Gregg, Lew Tapp; Jack Jones, Don Welsh, Les Lievesley; Ernie Steele, Fred Beedall, George Stabb, Albert Hutchinson, Morton 'Monty' Morgan; Manager; Frank Brown.
Argyle (2-3-5): Harry Cann; Harry Roberts, Tommy Black; Archie Gorman, Dave Hill, Reg Bungay; Jack Demellweek, Frank Sloan, Eugene 'Miffy' Melaniphy, Len Featherby, Jack Vidler; Manager: Robert Jack.

Joyous scenes were witnessed at Plainmoor, as home supporters invaded the pitch to celebrate Torquay United's first-ever championship victory in the thirteenth year of the triangular competition. The Magpies had overcome Exeter City 5-1 in the semi-final, and followed this up with a thoroughly deserved win over a strong Plymouth Argyle side. Long after the home side had reached the sanctuary of the dressing room, after running the gauntlet of their back-slapping fans, the cheering crowd remained behind and did not disperse until dusk fell. Before they left, United chairman Charles Dear made a speech on behalf of 'his boys' reiterating what a proud moment this was in the club's history.

The Pilgrims knew they faced an uphill task when they went behind within ten minutes of the kick-off. Ernie Steele rounded defenders Reg Bungay and Tommy Black, then pulled the ball back across the face of the goal for fellow winger 'Monty' Morgan to hoist it over the body of advancing 'keeper Harry Cann.

Left: *Monty Morgan opens the scoring.* Right: *Two-goal Ernie Steele.*

Morgan was in the thick of the action again after eighteen minutes, when he was hauled down in the box by wing-half Archie Gorman. The referee immediately pointed to the spot and centre forward George Stabb, who had already had a goal disallowed for offside, suffered further disappointment when Harry Cann anticipated his intentions and pulled off a brilliant save, diving low to his left.

The home fans were left to ponder during the interval whether this miss had let Argyle off the hook, but within ten minutes of the restart, the Magpies had wrapped up the game with two more well-taken goals – the elusive Ernie Steele showed great opportunism to sink the visitors with a lightning double-strike. Firstly, he popped up to finish off a stylish passing movement with Fred Beedal and George Stabb, then increased his side's lead further when Albert Hutchinson floated a free-kick to the far post. The ball was half-cleared before falling to Steele, who hammered the ball past the powerless Cann. Shell-shocked Argyle fought hard to get back in the game, but came up against a defence superbly marshalled by Don Welsh. United's centre half would later be capped for England and lead Charlton Athletic out in two Wembley FA Cup finals, but the reception of the Torquay fans at the final whistle all but matched these illustrious occasions. After all, lowly Torquay had triumphed in Devon's very own version of the cup final!

It proved to be 'lucky thirteen' for United, whose previous struggles in the competition were put firmly behind them. Having broken the domination of their two derby rivals, they continued the winning habit to snatch the championship on three consecutive occasions.

An extraordinary row broke out between two local football reporters, following Exeter City's defeat by Torquay United in the semi-final of the Devon Professional Championship in April 1933. Bearing in mind Exeter City's preoccupation with the promotion race, 'Nomad' pointed out in the 'Express & Echo' that 'United could not help winning' because: 'From the first kick it was evident that the Grecians were not taking the game at all seriously. They played at rather less than half speed throughout, and quite rightly failed to take any risks which might have jeopardised their chances of promotion. I have never seen greater conservation of energy on a football field than Exeter showed last night, and this explains why the home side was beaten by three goals to one'. 'Touch' retaliated strongly in the 'Torbay Football Herald' to the charge that a virtually full-strength Exeter had not been concerned about winning the derby and reminded his readers that 'Nomad' (meaning 'a voice in the wilderness') was an apt name for his press colleague: 'I'm telling you straight from the shoulder that your argument is one of the most unsporting I have ever seen or want to see ... I notice that you are still counting your promotion chickens. I only hope you won't find your eggs addled'.

PLYMOUTH ARGYLE 6 EXETER CITY 4
DEVON PROFESSIONAL CHAMPIONSHIP SEMI-FINAL, 28 SEPTEMBER 1938

Argyle (2-3-5): Harry Cann; John Murray, Jimmy Rae; Archie Gorman, Sam Kirkwood, Sammy Black; Jimmy Hunter, Harry Lane, Bill Hullett, Jackie Smith, Alec Dyer; Manager: Jack Tresadern.
City (2-3-5): Vince Blore; Bill Brown, John Little; John Shadwell, Bill Fellowes, Jack Angus; Alex Turnbull, Walter Bussey, Harry Bowl, Richard 'Digger' Ebdon, Len Rich; Manager: Jack English.

A sparse Wednesday afternoon crowd at Home Park, reported by the *Western Morning News* to be 'fewer than 1,000', witnessed the highest aggregate score in the history of the competition, as the old soccer rivals battled for the honour of meeting Torquay United in the final. City were hoping to avenge a 5-3 defeat, inflicted at Home Park a month earlier, when the teams had met in a friendly to raise money for the Football League Jubilee Fund. For this match, Argyle made changes in defence and fielded an experimental forward line. They played delightful fast-flowing football in the first half and completely overran the Exeter defence. After the interval, the Pilgrims made the mistake of sitting on a four-goal lead and almost lost their grip on the tie, as City unbelievably stormed back into contention.

Argyle's danger man in the first half was left-winger Alec Dyer. The former Crewe Alexandra player gave a dazzling display, and his pinpoint crosses created four goals before he got on the score sheet himself. Bill Fellowes, normally a half-back for City, had been switched to centre half for this match. He looked distinctly uncomfortable in the role of 'stopper', especially in the air. The home side went on the attack straight from the kick-off, Dyer's centre eluded Fellowes, and was met by inside-left Jackie Smith to give Argyle an early lead. City quickly hit back to level the scores through winger Len Rich, but for the next half hour, Argyle 'keeper Harry Cann was rarely troubled by the visitors, as Alec Dyer's tantalising runs posed a constant threat to City. He set up two goals for centre forward Bill Hullett (who had already collected two League hat-tricks that season) and one for inside-right Harry Lane, then skipped through the shell-shocked City defence to shoot past 'keeper Vince Blore and give Argyle a seemingly unassailable 5-1 lead at the break.

The Grecians came out fighting in the second half, determined to reduce the gap. Leading scorer Harry Bowl signalled a recovery, with a superb double-strike to put pressure on an increasingly shaky Argyle defence. However, Plymouth's nerves were settled when Harry Lane fired home his second goal to give the home side a three-goal cushion, with the score at 6-3. This deficit did nothing to deter an Exeter team, desperate to restore some professional pride. Their cause was helped by Argyle full-back Jimmy Rae, who had the misfortune to turn the ball into his own net when attempting to clear a corner. Argyle weathered the storm during the last few minutes, and clung onto their two-goal

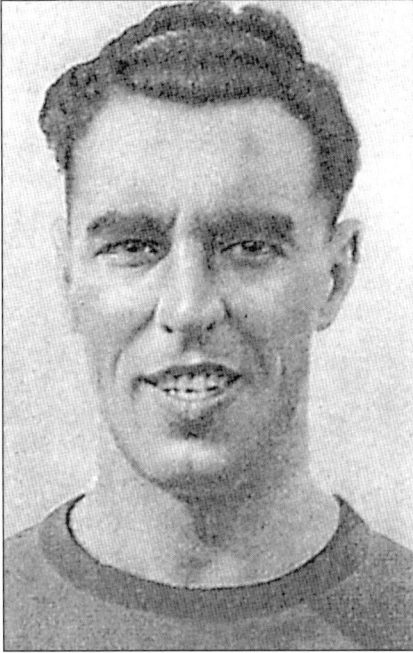

Left: *Bill Hullet – two goals for Argyle.* Right: *Harry Bowl – two goals for City.*

advantage until the final whistle in a thoroughly entertaining derby, which had deserved better support from the local football-supporting public.

When the semi-final of the Devon Professional Championship had been completed, it was not uncommon for the finalists immediately to telephone the club that had received a bye, to decide at whose ground the final would be played. With a Devon County FA official on hand to ensure fair play, the caller would spin a coin and the receiver would have the honour of calling heads or tails! In 1952, Plymouth Argyle went on to defeat Exeter City in the final after overcoming Torquay United with the help of a coin! As Home Park had no floodlights at this time, the semi-final took place in March on a Monday afternoon, kicking-off at 5 p.m. The match ended in a 1-1 draw and, as darkness was falling, the referee agreed that the light was too poor to enable extra-time to be played. The team managers were then called upon to decide the tie on the spin of a coin! Jimmy Rae tossed and Eric Webber called incorrectly!

TORQUAY UNITED 2 PLYMOUTH ARGYLE 2
DEVON PROFESSIONAL CHAMPIONSHIP FINAL, 5 OCTOBER 1938

United (2-3-5): Phil Joslin; Bert Head, Albert 'Bob' Keeton; Harold Cothliff, Albert Hutchinson, Bill Coley; Roy Fursdon, Herbert Dyer, Jack Haycox, Andy Brown, Stan Pope; Manager: Alf Steward.
Argyle (2-3-5): Harry Cann; Sam Kirkwood, George Silk; W.L. Roberts, Jimmy Clarke, Tommy Ryan; Jimmy Hunter, Harry Lane, Jack Vidler, Henry Brown, Alec Dyer; Manager: Jack Tresadern.

The last championship final to be played before the Second World War produced a high-class game, packed with thrills and good football, which ended with honours even at Plainmoor. Holders Plymouth Argyle made several changes from the side which had overcome Exeter City 6-4 in the semi-final, and the Second Division outfit were, as always, firm favourites to beat their rivals from the basement League.

The Magpies lost the toss and faced a stiff breeze in the first half, but quickly settled into their stride and boldly took the game to their opponents. Abandoning their normal 'kick and rush' style, which was popular with the supporters but useless when playing against the wind, they produced quality

Jack Vidler missed a vital penalty.

passing and movement, which kept Argyle penned in their own half for long periods and forced them to defend grimly against a lively attack. Just when it seemed that the visitors would survive their ordeal until the break without conceding a goal, United turned their territorial advantage into goals with two strikes in quick succession just before the break. Winger Roy Fursdon, a recent signing from Tiverton Town, had a hand in both. He set up the opener with a pass to centre forward Jack Haycox, who gave 'keeper Harry Cann no chance with a superbly-struck drive along the ground, which nestled in the corner of the net. To the delight of the Plainmoor faithful, Fursdon then linked up with inside forward Herbert Dyer, who extended Torquay's lead and deservedly confirmed the home team's superiority.

Early in the second half, Argyle had a wonderful opportunity to pull a goal back when they were awarded a penalty. To the relief of the home side, centre forward Jack Vidler blazed the spot-kick well wide of the post. To their credit, the Pilgrims did not let their heads drop following this disappointment, and Torquay 'keeper Phil Joslin was forced to make several fine saves to deny an attack that was beginning to show its class. Argyle got their just reward for some fine play mid-way through the second half, when left-winger Alec Dyer connected with Jimmy Hunter's cross-field pass to beat Joslin with a flying header. Right-winger Jimmy Hunter was now exerting a telling influence on this match. His marker, Bob Keeton, was feeling somewhat below par, having undergone dental extractions earlier that day. With thirteen minutes remaining, the Torquay full-back was powerless to prevent Hunter slipping a pass to his inside partner, Harry Lane, who equalised with a powerful shot from an oblique angle, which went in off the underside of the bar. Extra time was not played, due to failing light, nor a replay arranged, therefore the title was shared by the two clubs until the competition made a welcome return in peacetime, seven years later.

EXETER CITY 1 PLYMOUTH ARGYLE 2
DEVON PROFESSIONAL CHAMPIONSHIP FINAL, 3 MAY 1950
(ATTENDANCE 8,963)

City (2-3-5): Barney Singleton; Cyril Johnstone, Jim Clark; Peter Fallon, Ray Goddard, Fred Davey; Bill Harrower, Dennis Hutchins, Archie Smith, Angus Mackay, Charlie McClelland; Manager: George Roughton.
Argyle (2-3-5): Les Major; Paddy Ratcliffe, Pat Jones; Neil Dougall, Jack 'Jumbo' Chisholm, John Porteous; Gordon Astall, Frank Squires, Eric Bryant, George Willis, Alex Govan; Manager: Jimmy Rae.

The Devon Professional Championship final had a special presentation ceremony, when Plymouth Argyle and Exeter City fought for a trophy donated by Torquay United. For many years prior to this date, the competition had merely been marked by players receiving medals. Plymouth Argyle were still licking their wounds, having just been relegated to join up with Exeter City and Torquay United for the first time since 1930. City sports reporter 'Exonian', reporting on this final in the *Western Morning News*, correctly forecast that, on this display, the Pilgrims 'will be among the leaders in the less exacting Third Division grade next season'.

The Grecians survived a battering in a goal-less first half. Goalkeeper Barney Singleton made some inspired saves, and centre half Ray Goddard was in outstanding form against his former club. After the interval, City had a brief spell of brilliance, against the run of play, and took the lead after fifty-seven minutes with a well-worked move. A clearance by full-back Jim Clark was picked up by Charlie McClelland. The left-winger jinked his way past two defenders and made an inch-perfect cross for striker Archie Smith to head in at the near post. Moments later, City had a great opportunity to increase their lead, when Angus Mackay outpaced left-back Pat Jones and lobbed the ball to the unmarked Dennis Hutchins. With only 'keeper Les Major to beat, the inside forward headed just over the bar from eight yards. Following this near miss, Argyle regained the initiative, and half-back Neil Dougall levelled the scores with a swerving shot from 25 yards which deceived Singleton. From this point onwards, there was only one team in it, and it came as no surprise when Argyle snatched the lead. Winger 'Flash' Gordon Astall lived up to his nickname and outstripped the City defence, before reaching the byline and hitting a low cross into the box. The ball reached fellow winger Alex Govan, whose first time shot from close range was a winner all the way.

Skipper Jumbo Chisholm led his triumphant team off the pitch, and was the first recipient of the new trophy, which was presented to him by the Revd Jesse Browne, chairman of the Devon County FA. However, if the Pilgrims thought they were going to have a easy ride on their return to the Third Division (South), they were in for a rude awakening. On their return

Alex Govan scored the winner.

to St James Park in February 1951, they were beaten by the odd goal in five in the first League meeting between the two teams for twenty years.

Author George Orwell could not have made it up, but in the year in which his futuristic novel, '1984', is set, Devon County FA resurrected the Devon Professional Bowl tournament, after a lapse of ten years, and contacted the last winners, Exeter City, for the return of the trophy. Embarrassed City officials admitted that they had no idea where the bowl was. The County FA secretary was not amused and could be forgiven for thinking that a club, not renowned for its bulging trophy cabinet, would have the silverware proudly on display in a place of honour at the ground. The club launched an immediate investigation at St James Park and, to their relief, the mystery was solved by the groundsman, Sonny Clarke. He produced the prized asset from the depths of his shed, which apparently doubled as the Grecians' very own Room 101!

PLYMOUTH ARGYLE 4 TORQUAY UNITED & EXETER CITY 2
DEVON PROFESSIONAL CHAMPIONSHIP FINAL, 5 MAY 1960
(ATTENDANCE 5,289)

Argyle (2-3-5): Geoff Barnsley; Reg Wyatt, Reg Fulton; Johnny Williams, Richard Gray, John Newman; Peter Anderson, Alex Jackson, George Kirby, Jim McAnearney, Bill Wright; Joint Managers: Neil Dougall & George Taylor.
Combined XI (2-3-5): Alan Jones (Exeter); Colin Bettany (Torquay), Les McDonald (Exeter); Arnold Mitchell (Exeter), George Northcott (Torquay), Jimmy Thompson (Exeter); Larry Baxter (Torquay), Graham Rees (Exeter), Tommy Northcott (Torquay), Graham Bond (Torquay), Gordon Dale (Exeter); Joint Managers: Eric Webber & Frank Broome.

Westcountry soccer fans converged on Home Park to witness a unique event. The Devon County FA sanctioned an imaginative change to the Devon Professional Championship, and temporarily ditched the traditional knock-out format of the triangular tournament. This innovation meant that, for the very first time, players from all three local clubs were on view in a competitive match. The cream of Devon's footballers served up a real end-of-season treat for the occasion and, in a storming finish, Plymouth Argyle twice came from

Peter Anderson wraps up the game for Argyle.

behind to score three times in the last ten minutes, thus snatching victory from the jaws of defeat, against a side comprising five Torquay United and six Exeter City players!

The Combined XI rattled their Second Division opponents during the opening phase of play, with veteran City winger Gordon Dale the star of the improvised forward line. Tommy Northcott, Torquay's top marksman in a season that had brought the Plainmoor club promotion, gave his side a deserved lead after fourteen minutes. The bustling leader of the attack fired home after latching onto a mistake by seventeen-year-old part-time professional Richard Gray, drafted into the side at late notice because of an injury to centre half Gordon Fincham. Argyle continued to be outplayed, and could count themselves fortunate to go in at the interval only one down, after Torquay forward Graham Bond hit the bar and 'keeper Geoff Barnsley made a splendid save to deny Exeter wing-half Jimmy Thompson. After the restart, the Pilgrims began to reproduce the form which had produced a bright finish to a relegation-haunted season. Forward Alex Jackson hit an upright before Argyle levelled the scores. From Bill Wright's corner kick, George Kirby rose above the defence to beat Exeter 'keeper Alan Jones with a fine header. The home crowd's joy was short-lived, however, as Torquay's Graham Bond darted into the box to pounce on a defensive error after seventy-one minutes to restore the lead for the combined side.

With the minutes ticking away, the championship appeared to have slipped beyond Argyle's grasp, but they thrilled their supporters by launching a spirited comeback that left the opposition reeling. Alex Jackson rammed in the equaliser ten minutes from the close. Two minutes later, winger Bill Wright coolly headed the home side in front from close range. Argyle refused to sit on their slender lead and a rampant attack surged back for more. On the stroke of time, winger Peter Anderson snatched Argyle's fourth goal. Remarkably, in the final passage of play, a one-goal deficit had been turned into an unlikely two-goal victory for the tenacious Pilgrims!

When Exeter manager Jim Iley got the dreaded vote of confidence from his club chairman in 1985, it came as no surprise when he was sacked three months later! The dismissal brought a storm of protest from club supporters, who organized a petition, and two dozen pro-Iley picketers stood outside St James Park, hoping to persuade supporters to boycott the Devon Bowl semi-final against Torquay. They must have wondered whether the effort was really necessary, as the match only attracted 564 spectators. At times, the chanting protestors outside the ground made more noise than the paying customers, as the home side edged to a win with the only goal of the match!

TORQUAY UNITED & EXETER CITY 2 PLYMOUTH ARGYLE 1
DEVON PROFESSIONAL CHALLENGE BOWL FINAL, 19 APRIL 1961
(ATTENDANCE 1,580)

Combined XI (2-3-5): Mervyn Gill (Torquay); Colin Bettany (Torquay), Les McDonald (Exeter); Dave Hancock (Torquay), Alan Smith (Torquay), Mike Eckersall (Torquay); Graham Bond (Exeter), Geoff Cox (Torquay), Tommy Northcott (Torquay), Ray Carter (Exeter), Gordon Dale (Exeter); Managers: Eric Webber and Glen Wilson.
Plymouth Argyle (2-3-5): John Leiper; George Robertson, Bryce Fulton; Johnny Williams, Gordon Fincham, John Newman; Peter Anderson, Wilf Carter, George Kirby, Alex Jackson, Ken Maloy; Manager: Neil Dougall.

For the first time, the competition was referred to as the Devon Professional Challenge Bowl, as a combined team of Third and Fourth Division players from Torquay United and Exeter City respectively, wrested the championship from Second Division Plymouth Argyle, thus gaining revenge for their defeat the previous season. This proved to be the last time a combined side featured in the competition before it was decided to revert to a three-cornered fight for the trophy.

City wing-half Arnold Mitchell was selected for the match, but was ruled out with laryngitis and replaced by United's Mike Eckersall – which meant that only four Exeter representatives took part in the game: Les McDonald, Gordon Dale

Alan Smith – an unlucky own goal for Argyle's equalizer.

Tommy Northcott scored the decider from the spot.

and former United players, Graham Bond and Ray Carter. Plymouth fielded their strongest side, with the exception of forward Jimmy McAnearney, who was unavailable for selection due to a family bereavement.

The Second Division outfit looked slicker from the outset, while their opponents understandably took time to settle. Fast, open football ensued, and there were plenty of goalmouth incidents and narrow escapes for both defences, before two own goals were scored by the opposing centre halves. Five minutes before the interval, Gordon Fincham turned a cross from Gordon Dale past a stunned John Leiper in the Argyle goal. Midway through the second half, Alan Smith returned the compliment, when he attempted to whip the ball off the toes of striker Wilf Carter, and inadvertently beat Mervyn Gill. Both sides then went all out for the winner, with impressive displays from both teams' centre forwards. Argyle's George Kirby skimmed the woodwork with a blistering shot, headed against the crossbar, then had another effort well saved by Mervyn Gill. For the Combined XI, Tommy Northcott made a great chance for Graham Bond, which went begging, then hit a tremendous drive which brought the best save of the night out of John Leiper.

Just as the match appeared to be heading for an honourable draw, the tireless Northcott's persistence finally paid off when an Argyle defender's hand intercepted a pass intended for the striker as he bore down on goal. The referee had no hesitation in awarding a penalty and Tommy immediately assumed responsibility for the outcome of the match. Picking up the ball, he placed it on the spot and drove the ball past Leiper, sealing a dramatic victory with only five minutes remaining of a thrilling encounter.

TORQUAY UNITED 2 PLYMOUTH ARGYLE 3
(EXTRA-TIME PLAYED)
DEVON PROFESSIONAL CHALLENGE BOWL FINAL, 11 MAY 1966

United (2-3-5): Mike Turner; Eric Burgess, Tony Hellin; Geoff Cox, Reg Wyatt, Trevor Wolstenholme; Mickey Somers, John Evans, Robin Stubbs, Tommy Northcott, Gerry King; Manager: Frank O'Farrell.
Argyle (2-3-5): John Leiper; Tony Rounsevell, John Hore; Johnny Williams, Andy Nelson, Norman Piper; Dave Corbett, Tony Brimacombe, Mike Bickle, Keith Etheridge, Cliff Jackson; Manager: Derek Ufton.

This championship final was the third game in three days at Plainmoor, and could not have been come at a more inopportune moment for Torquay United. Pressing for promotion from the Fourth Division, a Monday night win over Notts County had taken them to the top of the table. On Tuesday they joined forces with Argyle to play against Arsenal in a testimonial match for popular United goalkeeper Terry Adlington, whose career had been brought to an end by a finger injury. Now, twenty-four hours later, several of the same players lined up against each other in a stamina-sapping game for the Devon Professional Bowl, which was eventually decided in extra time.

Argyle striker Mike Bickle started where he had left off the night before, when he had produced a late two-goal burst to sink the Gunners 5-4. He quickly proved to the Torquay crowd that this performance was no fluke. After fifteen minutes, he got the better of his marker, former Plymouth defender Reg Wyatt, and took a pass from inside left Keith Etheridge to fire the visitors into the lead. Etheridge himself got on the score sheet after the break, when he beat 'keeper Mike Turner from close range in the sixty-seventh minute. Plymouth's name looked certain to be on the trophy, as a lethargic United team didn't look capable of reducing the deficit. The game was drifting towards its conclusion, when a late Torquay rally suddenly brought the result into doubt. With five minutes of normal time remaining, striker Robin Stubbs turned a cross past John Leiper. With the Gulls' fans suddenly scenting a sniff of a chance, they urged their team to make one last concerted effort. Moments later, Argyle conceded a corner under pressure. A swinging cross from Mickey Somers was met by Tommy Northcott, who headed in a sensational last-ditch equalizer.

The match moved into extra time, and Robin Stubbs almost produced a fairy-tale ending to United's fightback when he crashed a tremendous shot against the bar. The Pilgrims gradually regained their composure and, seven minutes from the end, snatched the winner with a goal from amateur forward Tony Brimacombe. He finished off good work by rising star Norman Piper, who had just been selected, along with another Argyle youngster, Richard Reynolds, for the England Youth World Cup squad.

Members of the United squad took it easy after this game, and three days later manager Frank O'Farrell accompanied some of his players to Wembley to

Robin Stubbs sparked a United revival which took the match into extra-time.

see former Argyle striker Mike Trebilcock in his finest hour, scoring two brilliant goals in Everton's FA Cup final win over Sheffield Wednesday. The following Saturday, a goal-less draw at Darlington was enough to leave the Gulls in third place and secure their passage to the Third Division.

The introduction of promotion play-offs and automatic relegation for the bottom club in the League produced a nail-biting climax to the 1986/87 season, with Plymouth Argyle missing out on possible elevation to the First Division, and Torquay United retaining their League place by the skin of Bryn the police-dog's teeth! No sooner had these minor matters been decided, than thoughts turned to the competition for the Devon Bowl. The clubs had hoped to hold over the tournament until the beginning of the following season, but, under Devon County FA regulations, this would have incurred a £200 fine. The semi-final between Exeter City and Torquay United was therefore arranged at twenty-four hours' notice and played on a Monday afternoon at the Cat & Fiddle training ground at Clyst St Mary. The switch was made from St James Park to avoid policing costs, which the previous season had amounted to £1,300 when only 600 people had attended. Small wonder the competition was abandoned for six years, after Exeter brushed aside the challenge of Torquay and Plymouth to win the trophy for the third year in a row!

TORQUAY UNITED 4 PLYMOUTH ARGYLE 2
DEVON PROFESSIONAL CHALLENGE BOWL FINAL, 4 MAY 1971
(ATTENDANCE 2,339)

United (4-3-3): Andy Donnelly; Ian Twitchin, Dick Edwards, Derek Harrison, Bill Kitchener; Mal Lucas, Mickey Cave, Tommy Mitchinson; Bruce Stuckey (sub: Cliff Jackson), John Rudge, Alan Welsh; Manager: Allan Brown.
Argyle (4-2-4): Jim Furnell; Steve Davey, Bobby Saxton, Dave Provan, Alan Harris; Mike Dowling, David Burnside (sub: Derek Rickard); Trevor Shepherd, Jim Hinch, Keith Allen, Don Hutchins; Manager: Ellis Stuttard.

Top scorer John Rudge passed a late fitness test and scored a hat-trick, as the Gulls twice came from behind to retain the Devon Bowl in this keenly contested struggle for local soccer supremacy. An extra-time victory completed a remarkable treble for United, who had already humbled Argyle twice in the League – a feat accomplished for the first time and which they have never yet repeated!

A lively opening saw both 'keepers fully extended, as the fierce rivalry between the sides produced an exciting, attacking game. In the thirty-third minute, the home fans were infuriated by the referee's decision to turn down a penalty appeal, after Argyle defender Bobby Saxton appeared to manhandle

Hat-trick hero John Rudge leads United off the pitch, followed by skipper Mal Lucas clutching the Devon Bowl.

130

Alan Welsh as he ran onto a through ball from Mal Lucas. Five minutes later, the visitors took the lead, when striker Jim Hinch nipped in between 'keeper Andy Donnelly and central defender Derek Harrison to flash in a header from a Dave Provan cross. The Gulls got a lucky break after the interval, when full-back Alan Harris was harshly judged to have handled a cross, driven at him by winger Bruce Stuckey. John Rudge had beaten Argyle 'keeper Jim Furnell from the spot in the League match at Home Park on Boxing Day, and again made no mistake, hitting the penalty high into the right-hand corner of the net. Argyle came closest to winning the game in normal time, when Jim Hinch brought the best out of Andy Donnelly with a blistering 40-yard drive, which was tipped over the bar.

Argyle appeared to have their hands on the trophy, when they regained the lead in the eighth minute of extra time. Andy Donnelly went down to block a shot from Jim Hinch, and substitute Derek Rickard promptly stabbed home the rebound. Torquay fought back determinedly and moved up a gear during the second period of extra time. Two minutes after the restart, John Rudge robbed Don Hutchins on the byline and equalized from an acute angle, craftily chipping over the head of Furnell. Former Argyle winger, and United substitute, Cliff Jackson had a goal disallowed for offside, before the Gulls went ahead for the first time with the best move of the match in the 112th minute. Midfield playmaker Tommy Mitchinson stroked in a ball, which was back-headed by Cliff Jackson into the path of Alan Welsh, who lobbed over the advancing Furnell. With seconds to go, Torquay were toying with the opposition, and Jim Furnell was left totally exposed, as Alan Welsh drew him to the near post, before rolling the ball to John Rudge, who tapped in his third goal and earned himself the match ball as a memento. Joyous supporters swarmed onto the pitch to salute the victors, as skipper Mal Lucas paraded the trophy before leading his triumphant team to the dressing-room for a champagne celebration.

After an absence of six years, the Devon Bowl returned by popular demand in 1993. The folly of playing the tournament at the end of the season, when promotion and relegation issues had still to be decided was not repeated. A pre-season round-robin event was introduced to replace the familiar knock-out format. Straight away there were problems, when Torquay United protested about the Devon County FA rule that only allowed contract players to take part and excluded trialists. However, the club had overlooked the fact that the competition had been set up in the first place because the professional clubs were prevented from playing their first team in the Devon Senior Cup, as they employ more than three contracted players. The red tape row was therefore easily resolved with words to the effect: 'Rules is rules!'

EXETER CITY 3 TORQUAY UNITED 0
DEVON PROFESSIONAL CHALLENGE BOWL FINAL, 9 MAY 1974
(ATTENDANCE 796)

City (4-3-3): Bob Wilson; Campbell Crawford, Jimmy Giles, Hedley Steele, Brian Joy; John Neale, Graham Parker, Dave Gibson; Bobby Hodge, Keith Bowker, Ken Wallace; Manager: John Newman.
United (4-2-4): Mike Mahoney; Clint Boulton, Derek Harrison, Dave Stocks (sub: Peter Bastow), Phil Sandercock; James De Garis, Eddie Rowles; Dave Kennedy, Bradley Beattie, Richard Goslin, Steve Morrall; Manager: Malcolm Musgrove.

The hardy souls who braved foul weather at St James Park to watch the climax to a season of mid-table mediocrity, at least had the satisfaction of seeing Exeter City win the Challenge Bowl for the first time in six years. In fact, the Grecians would retain custody of the trophy for a decade, as the competition was suspended the following season in favour of a one-off Devon Professional Five-a-Side tournament, sponsored by Texaco, which was won by Torquay United.

The final kicked off in torrential rain and buffeting winds. Pools of surface water quickly formed on the pitch, making conditions treacherous underfoot. Exeter survived early pressure and were fortunate not to go behind in the opening minutes. Winger Dave Kennedy met a cross on the far post and hit his shot well, but 'keeper Bob Wilson responded with a magnificent reflex save from point blank range. Newton Abbot schoolboy Richard Gosling, who had made his League debut for United two days earlier, also went close with a blistering 25-yard drive, which took a deflection before just clearing the bar. With the pitch starting to resemble a ploughed field, City gradually began to win the crucial midfield battle, with an outstanding performance from Graham Parker. He was Exeter's powerhouse and grafted tirelessly for the full ninety minutes. The Grecians deservedly went ahead a minute before the interval, when amateur Bobby Hodge showed the potential which would later earn him a full-time contract, with a defence-splitting pass to John Neale. The resultant cross found Dave Gibson, who had just been given a free transfer in City's end of season clear-out, and United's Player of the Year, 'keeper Mike Mahoney, was well beaten with a cracking shot into the corner of the net.

City increased their lead in the fifty-second minute, when Parker intercepted a pass and sent Ken Wallace away. The winger won a tussle with Clint Boulton, and appeared to pull down the full-back, but play was allowed to continue before he cut inside to beat Mahoney with a powerful cross-shot. Ten minutes from time, City put the result beyond doubt, when the non-stop Parker lost the defence with a blind-side run, and met a long cross from overlapping full-back Campbell Crawford to score with a superb diving header from 15 yards. Man of the Match Parker had every incentive to play well, as he had been put on the transfer list and was attracting interest from the Gulls. A bid of £2,500 had

Graham Parker – wanted by United.

already been turned down by the City board, but United manager Malcolm Musgrove was obviously convinced of the midfield dynamo's quality after this sparkling display, and successfully renewed his efforts to pursue his target and add him to the Plainmoor squad.

EXETER CITY 1 PLYMOUTH ARGYLE 1
(CITY WON 6-5 ON PENALTIES)
DEVON PROFESSIONAL BOWL FINAL, 13 MAY 1985
(ATTENDANCE 1,257)

City (4-4-2): Lee Smelt; Graham Kirkup, Nicky Marker, Jim McNichol, Keith Viney; Steve Harrower, Danny O'Shea, Martin Ling, Phil King; Kevin Smith (sub: Darren Clifford), Frank Howarth (sub: Dean Graves), Caretaker manager: John Hore.
Argyle (4-4-2): Geoff Crudgington (sub: Dave Philp); Gordon Nisbet, Clive Goodyear, Adrian Burrows, Chris Harrison; Russell Coughlin, Kevin Hodges, Kevin Summerfield (sub: John Uzzell), Leigh Cooper; Gordon Staniforth, Tommy Tynan; Manager: Dave Smith.

The Devon Professional Championship was revived after an absence of ten years, in the hope that the county's three League clubs might make a small profit instead of making annual donations to the Devon FA. The first final of the revitalized competition presented a selection crisis for Exeter City's acting manager, John Hore. Injury had already robbed him of club skipper, Gerry McElhinney, and the City attack was decimated through the enforced absence of forwards Trevor Morgan, Andy Rogers, and leading scorer and Player of the Year, Ray Pratt. The Grecians took to the field without a recognized striker and adopted a 'they shall

Tommy Tynan collects his 33rd goal of the season.

not pass' strategy. Therefore, it came as no surprise when the newly introduced penalty shoot-out came into operation after a scrappy, if eventful, final had failed to separate the teams after extra time.

Argyle had had by far the better opportunities to settle the outcome in normal time, which had eventually ended goal-less. Exeter entered extra time with only ten men, after Keith Viney was sent off for a foul on Russell Coughlin in the eighty-fifth minute. The game finally exploded into life in the 113th minute, when Argyle's Player of the Year, Tommy Tynan, grabbed his 33rd goal of the season to put Argyle deservedly ahead. Excellent close control by Gordon Staniforth, from a long through-ball, set up the opening for the prolific striker, who had time to pick his spot before driving the ball past 'keeper Lee Smelt. With three minutes remaining, City broke out of their defensive shell and Jim McNichol headed down a Martin Ling corner for substitute Dean Graves, a former Home Park apprentice, to crack in his first senior goal for the Grecians.

With the match ending all-square, Argyle 'keeper Dave Philp, a half-time replacement for Geoff Crudgington, was plunged into the spotlight for a nerve-wracking penalty shoot-out. He saved from Danny O'Shea to put his side ahead in the second of the first five rounds of spot-kicks. However, the advantage was lost when Adrian Burrows shot hopelessly wide in the fourth round to leave the penalty score level at 4-4. At the sudden death stage, City's Lee Smelt emerged as the hero of the night, when he pulled off a brilliant save to deny Gordon Nisbet. These last-gasp heroics secured the Bowl for Exeter, after Steve Harrower had beaten Dave Philp to put the Grecians 6-5 ahead. The result was a particularly satisfying moment for Exeter's caretaker-manager John Hore. During his playing career, he had served both clubs loyally, making 400 appearances for Argyle and a further 200 for City. He had been Plymouth's boss, before being dismissed seven months before this final, but was in for more disappointment a month later when he was passed over for a permanent position at Exeter, which was instead offered to Jim Iley.

In the aftermath of the tragedy at the Bradford City ground, when fire claimed the lives of many soccer fans in May 1985, it was announced that Westcountry players were to join forces to raise money for relatives of the victims, by staging a special charity match. A select side, comprising players from Plymouth Argyle, Exeter City and Torquay United, took on a Saltash United XI at Home Park. The game was the brainchild of Tavistock mayor Robin Fenner, who launched an appeal in conjunction with other mayors in the area, with all proceeds going to the Bradford City Disaster Fund. Lending his support to the idea, Argyle manager Dave Smith summed up the feelings of many in the game when he told the 'Western Morning News': 'When I think that my wife was sat in that stand five weeks ago, it brings it all home to you'.

PLYMOUTH ARGYLE 2 EXETER CITY 4
DEVON PROFESSIONAL BOWL FINAL, 7 MAY 1986,
(ATTENDANCE 2,340)

Argyle (3-5-2): Geoff Crudgington; Gordon Nisbett, Clive Goodyear (sub: John Uzzell), Leigh Cooper; John Matthews, Kevin Summerfield, Kevin Hodges, Russell Coughlin, Garry Nelson; Tommy Tynan (sub: Darren Rowbotham), John Clayton; Manager: Dave Smith.
City (3-5-2): John Shaw; John Impey, Aidan McCaffrey, Keith Viney; Steve Harrower, Nicky Marker, Martin Ling, Gary Jackson, Phil King; Tony Kellow (sub: Ian Wadsworth), Ray Pratt; Manager: Colin Appleton.

The mood in the two camps couldn't have been more different for this end-of-season final. Plymouth Argyle's players were celebrating promotion to the Second Division, and had brought their best suits along to Home Park, as they were invited to attend a civic reception in their honour later that night. In contrast, Exeter City's thoughts were focused on a fixture between Peterborough and Rochdale, which was taking place at the same time as the game. The outcome of that match would decide whether they would be accompanying neighbours Torquay United in seeking re-election to the Football League. If the Grecians had shown the same commitment in their League programme as they proceeded to demonstrate against their derby rivals, perhaps they would not have found themselves in such an awkward situation!

Plymouth were seeking revenge, having been eliminated from the Football League Cup at the start of the season by Exeter, but found themselves facing an uphill task, after the visitors took the lead after just eighty-five seconds. Argyle 'keeper Geoff Crudgington could only parry a shot from Steve Harrower into the path of Gary Jackson, who swept in the rebound. Crudgington was in trouble again shortly before half time, when he handled the ball outside the area. Tony Kellow crashed his free-kick past the defensive wall to give the Grecians a two-goal cushion at the interval.

Substitutes Darren Rowbotham and John Uzzell, who had both turned out for Argyle reserves at Bristol City during the afternoon, found themselves in action again during the second half, as manager Dave Smith tried to turn the tide. Russell Coughlin reduced the arrears from the penalty spot in the sixty-second minute, after Garry Nelson had been upended in the box by Tony Kellow. Twelve minutes later, the Argyle defence came to a standstill, waiting for an offside decision which never came, as Steve Harrower ran onto a through-ball from Nicky Marker and slotted the ball past the advancing Crudgington. John Clayton pulled one back with a seventy-eighth minute header, but any fears that that the Lord Mayor might be kept waiting by the addition of extra time were swept away three minutes from time, when Nicky Marker crossed from the right and Ray Pratt struck home from close range, ensuring Exeter's one bright spot of the season!

As the Argyle team dashed away from Home Park to cry into their champagne,

Steve Harrower scored City's third goal

Exeter heard the news that they had been dreading. Rochdale's late equaliser at Peterborough had pulled the Dale clear of the bottom four, leaving the Grecians with an anxious appointment at the Football League's annual meeting to decide their fate. Luckily, both they and Torquay emerged with their League status still intact!

The Eric Johnson benefit match at Plainmoor in May 1959, was in aid of the popular Torquay winger, whose career had been ended by injury. Coventry, his only other club, sent a side to face the cream of Devon, comprising five players from Torquay and three each from Exeter and Plymouth. The line-up provided a real treat for the 2,680 crowd, as the local favourites over-ran the Sky Blues, who had just won promotion from the Fourth Division. The match was marked by the virtuoso performance of goal ace Wilf Carter, who bagged five goals and laid on another for Tommy Northcott.

Devon XI (2-3-5): Mervyn Gill (Torquay) John Smith (Torquay), Les McDonald (Exeter); Colin Bettany (Torquay), Reg Wyatt (Plymouth), Arnold Mitchell (Exeter); Larry Baxter (Torquay), Wilf Carter (Plymouth), Tommy Northcott (Torquay), Gordon Dale (Exeter), Peter Anderson (Plymouth).

EXETER CITY 0 PLYMOUTH ARGYLE 3
DEVON PROFESSIONAL CHALLENGE BOWL, 9 AUGUST 1994,
(ATTENDANCE 2,432)

City (4-4-2): Andy Woodman; Scott Daniels, Jon Richardson, Mark Came,
Colin Anderson; Stuart Storer, Tony Thirlby, Russell Coughlin (sub: Mark
Cooper), Mark Gavin; Robbie Turner, Mickey Ross (sub: Richard Pears);
Manager: Terry Cooper.
Argyle (4-4-2): Ken Veysey; Marc Edworthy, Keith Hill, Andy Comyn, Ian Payne;
Wayne Burnett, Steve Castle, Martin Barlow, Craig Skinner; Kevin Nugent,
Mickey Evans; Manager: Peter Shilton.

After an absence of seven years, the Devon Professional Challenge Bowl was re-introduced in 1993, this time adopting a 'round robin' format. The competition was won by Argyle, who retained the trophy on this last occasion. The championship was decided in this enthralling encounter at a rain-sodden St James Park, following two games at Plainmoor in which Torquay United were defeated 1-2 by Exeter, then held to a 2-2 draw by Plymouth.

Hopes of an Argyle triumph looked extremely doubtful during the opening period, when the visitors' defence came under the cosh from a sizzling City attack. Exeter 'keeper Andy Woodman made a flying save in the fifth minute to tip over a 20-yard pile-driver from Martin Barlow, and was barely troubled again until midfielder Steve Castle beat him twice in six minutes, either side of the interval, to completely change the complexion of the match. It was virtually one-way traffic in the first half, as the Grecians outclassed their rivals. The pace of City flankers Stuart Storer and Mark Gavin tormented the Argyle defence, but the home side could not convert their superiority into goals. Debutant Ken Veysey had a charmed life in the Plymouth goal, as he somehow kept a clean sheet. Full-back Scott Daniels headed a Gavin free-kick narrowly over the bar after nine minutes. Moments later, Storer supplied a perfect cross to the far post, where the unmarked Mickey Ross missed a sitter from close range. Ross had further bad luck when a goal-bound header was cleared off the line, after it struck the knee of Martin Barlow. Fellow striker Robbie Turner was a constant threat, but failed to find the target with three headers from Russell Coughlin crosses. The Greens merely sat back, pinned in their own half, soaking up the pressure and could barely believe their luck when they sneaked ahead in a rare breakaway in the forty-second minute. Craig Skinner charged through from midfield, and his tame shot squirted into the path of Castle, who tapped in from the edge of the six-yard box. Three minutes into the second half, Castle struck again with another simple side-foot into the net, after City had conceded an unnecessary indirect free-kick just outside the penalty area.

Argyle now knew it was going to be their night and were much the better side, as the shell-shocked City team fell apart. The Grecians' misery was complete, when Mickey Evans scored a memorable solo effort, racing through

Steve Castle – two goals for Argyle.

from the halfway line to place his shot past Andy Woodman in the seventy-second minute. Plymouth strolled unopposed throughout the remainder of the game, and spurned several chances to turn what, at one point, had seemed an unlikely victory into a rout. Therefore, Plymouth, the winners of the first championship in 1923, also emerged victorious in what proved to be the last hurrah for this triangular tournament, which had spanned over seventy years of the twentieth century.

STATISTICS
Devon Professional Champions 1922-1995

Season	Winners	
1922/23	Plymouth Argyle	
1923/24	Plymouth Argyle	
1924/25	Plymouth Argyle	
1925/26	Exeter City	
1926/27	Exeter City	
1927/28	Exeter City	
1928/29	Plymouth Argyle	
1929/30	Plymouth Argyle	
1930/31	Plymouth Argyle	
1931/32	Plymouth Argyle	
1932/33	Plymouth Argyle	
1933/34	Plymouth Argyle	
1934/35	Torquay United	
1935/36	Torquay United	
1936/37	Torquay United	
1937/38	Plymouth Argyle	
1938/39	Plymouth and Torquay	(joint holders)*
1939/45	No Competition	
1945/46	Torquay United	
1946/47	No Competition	
1947/48	Torquay United	
1948/49	Plymouth Argyle	
1949/50	Plymouth Argyle	
1950/51	Plymouth Argyle	
1951/52	Plymouth Argyle	
1952/53	Torquay and Plymouth	(joint holders)*
1953/54	Torquay and Exeter	(joint holders)*
1954/55	Torquay and Exeter	(joint holders)*
1955/56	Plymouth Argyle	
1956/57	Plymouth Argyle	
1957/58	Torquay United	
1958/59	Exeter City	
1959/60	Plymouth Argyle	
1960/61	Torquay and Exeter Combined XI	
1961/62	Exeter City	
1962/63	Exeter City	
1963/64	Exeter City	
1964/65	Exeter City	
1965/66	Plymouth Argyle	
1966/67	Plymouth Argyle	
1967/68	Exeter City	
1968/69	Plymouth Argyle	
1969/70	Torquay United	
1970/71	Torquay United	
1971/72	Torquay United	
1972/73	Plymouth Argyle	
1973/74	Exeter City	
1974/84	No Competition	
1984/85	Exeter City	
1985/86	Exeter City	
1986/87	Exeter City	
1987/93	No Competition	
1993/94	Plymouth Argyle	
1994/95	Plymouth Argyle	

* Finals not played

Devon Professional Championship Results 1922-1995

Season

1922/23	SF	24 January	Torquay 1-0 Exeter	Plainmoor
	F	21 March	Plymouth 2-1 Torquay	Home Park
1923/24	SF	26 September	Exeter 1-0 Torquay	Plainmoor
	F	10 October	Plymouth 2-0 Exeter	Home Park
1924/25	SF	11 February	Exeter 7-1 Torquay	Plainmoor
	F	1st April	Plymouth 3-2 Exeter	St James Park
1925-26	SF	18 November	Plymouth 2-1 Torquay	Plainmoor
	F	10 March	Exeter 2-1 Plymouth	Home Park
1926/27	SF	16 February	Plymouth 5-1 Torquay	Plainmoor
	F	9 March	Exeter 3-1 Plymouth	St James Park
1927/28	SF	28 March	Torquay 0-0 Plymouth	Plainmoor
	Replay	16 April	Plymouth 1-0 Torquay	Home Park
	F	30 April	Exeter 4-2 Plymouth	St James Park
1928/29	SF[1]			
	F	24 April	Plymouth 3-2 Exeter	St James Park
1929/30	SF	16 April	Exeter 3-2 Torquay	St James Park
	F	30 April	Plymouth 2-0 Exeter	Home Park
1930/31	SF	23 April	Torquay 6-2 Exeter	Plainmoor
	F	29 April	Plymouth 5-1 Torquay	Home Park
1931/32	SF	13 April	Exeter 3-0 Torquay	St James Park
	F	20 April	Plymouth 2-1 Exeter	Home Park
1932/33	SF	5 April	Torquay 3-1 Exeter	St James Park
	F	24 April	Plymouth 3-1 Torquay	Home Park
1933/34	SF	13 September	Plymouth 3-1 Torquay	Plainmoor
	F	27 September	Plymouth 3-2 Exeter	St James Park
1934/35	SF	26 September	Torquay 5-1 Exeter	St James Park
	F	3 October	Torquay 3-0 Plymouth	Plainmoor
1935/36	SF	9 October	Plymouth 5-0 Exeter	Home Park
	F	13 November	Torquay 1-0 Plymouth	Home Park
1936/37	SF	21 April	Exeter 2-1 Plymouth	Home Park
	F	28 April	Exeter 1-1 Torquay	St James Park
	Replay	13 October	Torquay 1-0 Exeter	Plainmoor
1937/38	SF	1 December	Plymouth 5-2 Exeter	Home Park
	F	26 April	Plymouth 3-0 Torquay	Home Park
1938/39	SF	28 September	Plymouth 6-4 Exeter	Home Park
	F	5 October	Torquay 2-2 Plymouth	Plainmoor
1945/46	SF	10 April	Exeter 2-1 Plymouth	St James Park
	F	4 May	Torquay 4-0 Exeter	St James Park
1947/48	SF	5 April	Plymouth 2-1 Exeter	Home Park
	F	13 April	Torquay 1-0 Plymouth	Home Park
1948/49	SF	25 April	Torquay 3-1 Exeter	Plainmoor
	F	2 May	Plymouth 1-0 Torquay	Home Park
1949/50	SF	17 April	Exeter 3-0 Torquay	St James Park
	F	3 May	Plymouth 2-1 Exeter	St James Park
1950/51	SF	11 April	Plymouth 2-0 Exeter	St James Park
	F	2 May	Plymouth 2-1 Torquay	Plainmoor
1951/52	SF	31 March	*Plymouth 1-1 Torquay	Home Park
	F	2 May	Plymouth 1-0 Exeter	Home Park
1952/53	SF	29 April	Plymouth 4-1 Exeter	Home Park
	F[2]			
1953/54	SF	12 April	Torquay 2-1 Plymouth	Plainmoor
	F[2]			
1954/55	SF	3 May	Torquay 4-1 Plymouth	Plainmoor
	F[2]			

Season

1955/56	SF	7 March	Plymouth 4-0 Torquay	Home Park
	F	18 April	Plymouth 3-0 Exeter	Home Park
1956/57	SF	24 April	Plymouth 3-2 Torquay	Home Park
	F	2 May	Plymouth 4-2 Exeter	Home Park
1957/58	SF	26 March	Torquay 3-0 Plymouth	Home Park
	F	31 April	Torquay 3-0 Exeter	Plainmoor
1958/59	SF	4 April	Exeter 6-0 Plymouth	St James Park
	F	1 May	Exeter 2-1 Torquay	St James Park
1959/60	F	5 May	Plymouth 4-2 Torquay	Home Park
1960/61	F	19 April	Comb. XI 2-1 Plymouth	Plainmoor
1961/62	SF	20 March	Exeter 3-1 Plymouth	St James Park
	F	16 April	Exeter 2-0 Torquay	Plainmoor
1962/63	SF	24 April	Plymouth 2-1 Torquay	Plainmoor
	F	6 May	Exeter 1-0 Plymouth	St James Park
1963/64	SF[1]			
	F	28 April	Exeter 4-0 Plymouth	St James Park
1964/65	SF	25 March	Plymouth 3-0 Torquay	Home Park
	F	29 April	Exeter 1-0 Torquay	Home Park
1965/66	SF	3 May	Plymouth 3-2 Exeter	Home Park
	F	11 May	Plymouth 3-2 Torquay	Plainmoor
1966/67	SF	15 March	Plymouth 1-0 Exeter	St James Park
	F	8 May	Plymouth 2-1 Torquay	Home Park
1967/68	SF	19 March	Exeter 3-0 Torquay	St James Park
	F	13 May	Exeter 2-0 Plymouth	St James Park
1968/69	SF	17 February	Plymouth 1-0 Exeter	Home Park
	F	27 March	Torquay 0-0 Plymouth	Plainmoor
	Replay	2 May	Plymouth 2-0 Torquay	Home Park
1969/70	SF	25 April	Torquay 2-0 Plymouth	Home Park
	F	28 April	Torquay 1-0 Exeter	Plainmoor
1970/71	SF	9 March	Plymouth 2-1 Exeter	Home Park
	F	4 May	Torquay 4-2 Plymouth	Plainmoor
1971/72	SF	4 May	Exeter 2-1 Plymouth	St James Park
	F	8 May	Torquay 1-0 Exeter	Plainmoor
1972/73	SF	9 April	Exeter 2-0 Torquay	St James Park
	F	4 May	Plymouth 2-1 Exeter	Home Park
1973/74	SF[1]			
	F	9 May	Exeter 3-0 Plymouth	St James Park
1984/85	SF	29 April	Exeter 1-0 Torquay	St James Park
	F	13 May	Exeter 1-1 Plymouth 6-5 (penalty shootout)	St James Park
1985/86	SF	5 May	Exeter 3-0 Torquay	St James Park
	F	7 May	Exeter 4-2 Plymouth	Home Park
1986/87	SF	12 May	Exeter 5-1 Torquay	Clyst St Mary
	F	3 August	Exeter 1-0 Plymouth	St James Park
1993/94		31 July	Exeter 1-2 Torquay	St James Park
		4 August	Plymouth 3-0 Exeter	Home Park
		10 August	Torquay 0-1 Plymouth[3]	Plainmoor
1994/95		1 August	Torquay 1-2 Exeter	Plainmoor
		2 August	Torquay 2-2 Plymouth	Plainmoor
		9 August	Exeter 0-3 Plymouth[3]	St James Park

1 - Results not recorded
2 - Finals not played
3 - Plymouth won round robin tournament
* - Plymouth went through to final on the toss of a coin

5
'GYLES, GRECIANS & GULLS

Crad Evans proudly wears his Welsh amateur international cap, as he sits alongside the Devon Senior Cup with his Torquay team-mates in 1911. He was the first player to turn out for Plymouth, Exeter, and Torquay, although it would be another fifty years before anyone achieved the distinction of representing all three Devon clubs in the Football League.

Reg Jenkins – 'Local Legend' in football's Hall of Fame.

REG JENKINS (FORWARD)
born Millbrook 7 October 1938

When Reg Jenkins ran out at Plainmoor on 19 August 1961 to play in the opening match of the season against Crystal Palace, he made history by becoming the first player to complete a hat-trick of Football League appearances for all three Devon clubs.

The centre forward joined Argyle from Truro City in October 1957, and made his League debut at centre forward on 28 February 1959, in the 4-3 home win against Swindon. Jimmy Gauld notched a hat-trick, but Reg had to wait until his fourth appearance, before finding the net in the win over Chesterfield, as Argyle topped the table and romped to promotion as champions of the Third Division.

Opportunities to secure a regular place in the Second Division side were limited and, in December 1960, Reg joined Exeter City, then languishing near the foot of the Fourth Division. After helping the club to avoid re-election, he turned out regularly on the left wing the following season before moving to Torquay, who were promptly relegated to the Fourth Division.

Devon fans did not see the best of Reg. After three seasons at Plainmoor, former United winger Tony Collins swooped to take the burly forward to Rochdale. It was an inspired signing, and Reg became a folk hero to followers of the Dale. He scored 119 goals in 305 League outings, and helped the club climb out of the Fourth Division in the 1968/69 season. Thirty years later, Reg Jenkins was still remembered with awe by the Lancashire club's fans, who voted him the greatest player in Rochdale's history.

Club	Played	Devon Club Appearances			Goals		
		League	FAC	FLC	League	FAC	FLC
Argyle	1958-59	16	0	0	3	0	0
City	1959-61	20	0	0	6	0	0
United	1962-63	88	4	3	23	1	1
Total		124	4	3	32	1	1

DAVE HANCOCK (MIDFIELD)
born Exeter 24 July 1938

Dave Hancock was an outstanding rugby union prospect who gained international schoolboy honours for England while a pupil at Hele's School in Exeter, but he preferred soccer and joined Argyle as a junior in 1955, making his League debut the following season. Unable to command a first-team place, he went on loan to Gillingham, who failed to offer him a League chance, and his career finally took off when he joined Torquay in January 1959. The cultured wing-half established himself as a fixture in the side that won promotion, for the first time in the club's history, by finishing third in the Fourth Division in 1960.

Dave Hancock – a schoolboy rugby international.

Dave took part in another historic campaign, joining Exeter fifteen minutes before the transfer deadline for the run-in to the Grecians' first promotion success in 1964. He played in the last nine games of the season, including the crucial Easter derby against Torquay, and was selected at inside-left for City's last home game, where they gained an emphatic 6-1 victory over Chesterfield. This result virtually clinched the vital fourth and final promotion place, which booked Exeter's passage to the Third Division.

As well as being one of the elite band of players to have played for all three Devon clubs, Dave was also chosen to represent the combined Exeter & Torquay side that overcame Argyle's top Second Division team to win the 1961 Devon Professional Challenge Bowl.

Club	Played	Devon Club Appearances			Goals		
		League	FAC	FLC	League	FAC	FLC
Argyle	1956-57	2	0	0	0	0	0
United	1958-63	177	7	4	11	2	1
City	1963-64	40	1	2	3	0	1
Total		*219*	*8*	*6*	*14*	*2*	*2*

Peter Darke – versatile in defence or midfield.

PETER DARKE (DEFENDER)
born Exeter 21 December 1953

Spotted playing in same Exeter Schools team as future Argyle goalkeeper Peta Balac, Peter Darke also joined the club as an apprentice in December 1971, made his League debut at the age of eighteen and completed a century of first-team appearances for the Pilgrims. The versatile defender was a member of the squad that finished runners-up in the Third Division, earning promotion in 1975. The following year, he was loaned to Exeter and played a handful of games during City's successful promotion campaign, when the Grecians achieved second place and climbed out of the Fourth Division.

In March 1977, Mike Green, who had captained the Argyle promotion team, was appointed player-manager of Torquay, and Peter followed his former colleague to Plainmoor a few months later. It was the Gulls' Golden Jubilee year, which, unfortunately, coincided with a recurring theme in the club's history – financial crisis! The club's dream of celebrating their fiftieth season in the Football League by climbing out of the basement division failed to materialize. Yet, in times of financial constraint, Peter proved good value for money. By the time the curtain came down on his League career in 1979, he had filled every position in the back four and midfield for United.

| Club | Played | Devon Club Appearances | | | Goals | | |
		League	FAC	FLC	League	FAC	FLC
Argyle	1971-77	101	2	5	2	0	0
City	1976-77	5	0	0	0	0	0
United	1977-79	59	2	5	0	0	0
Total		165	4	10	2	0	0

FRED BINNEY (FORWARD)
born Plymouth 12 August 1946

Signed by Torquay in 1966, Fred Binney's arrival at Plainmoor from Launceston coincided with one of the most successful periods in the club's history, as they had just gained promotion from the Fourth Division under manager Frank O'Farrell. With strikers of the calibre of Robin Stubbs and Jim Fryatt on the club's books, Fred's chances to shine in the first team were limited, yet his promise was obvious, and his all-action bustling style endeared him to Gulls' supporters. Following a loan period at Exeter, when he notched 11 goals in 17 League matches, Fred joined the Grecians for £5,000, and became the only player in City's League history to become their top marksman for three consecutive seasons. Just before being voted Player of the Year

Fred Binney – never gave defenders a moment's peace.

in 1974, he was transferred to Brighton, then managed by Brian Clough. Fred scored 35 goals in 70 League appearances for the Seagulls, before injury impeded his progress during the club's promotion season to the Second Division.

After playing in America to regain full fitness, Fred finally got the chance to join his home city club in 1977. Argyle were struggling in the Third Division, but at the age of thirty-one, Fred proved he had lost none of his goal-scoring flair, and bettered his career average of a goal every two games. He was the natural choice for Player of the Year in 1979, having scored 26 goals in 42 League games. This was a fine swan-song for a tireless striker, who never gave defences a moment's peace. Fred moved on the following season to end his League career with Hereford, before embarking on a coaching career which included a return to St James Park under manager Colin Appleton in 1985.

Club	Played	Devon Club Appearances			Goals		
		League	FAC	FLC	League	FAC	FLC
United	1967-69	34	0	2	11	0	1
City	1969-73	177	5	7	90	1	7
Argyle	1977-79	71	2	7	39	0	3
Total		*282*	*7*	*16*	*140*	*1*	*11*

George Foster – Player of the Year for two Devon clubs.

GEORGE FOSTER
(CENTRAL DEFENDER)
born Plymouth 26 September 1956

Local boy George Foster became an Argyle apprentice in September 1974. He made a handful of first-team appearances in the forward line the following season, before spending a brief period on loan with Torquay, where he was used successfully as a striker. Returning to Home Park, he was converted to centre-back, and established himself as a regular choice, making over 200 appearances during the next four seasons. He was the fans' choice for the Player of the Year award in 1978 and 1980.

Loaned to Exeter, the first of only 28 games he played for the Grecians, was against the Pilgrims. His strong-tackling displays were so impressive that he earned the supporters' vote for Player of the Year in 1982, despite the fact that, by the time the award was made, he had returned to Argyle at the end of his loan period.

Considered surplus to requirements at Home Park, transfers took George first to Derby, and then to Mansfield. He proved that, even with his vast wealth of experience, he was still approaching his peak. Incredibly, he made over 400 appearances for the Stags, and captained their victorious Freight Rover Trophy team at Wembley in 1987. Two years later, he was appointed Mansfield player-manager, and has continued in the game in various coaching roles.

| Club | Played | Devon Club Appearances | | | Goals | | |
		League	FAC	FLC	League	FAC	FLC
Argyle	1974-81	212	10	19	6	0	0
United	1976	6	0	0	3	0	0
City	1981-82	28	0	0	0	0	0
Total		246	10	19	9	0	0

JOHN SIMS (FORWARD)
born Belper 14 August 1952

John Sims was a much-travelled striker, having played for Derby, Luton, Oxford, Colchester and Notts County, before arriving at Exeter in December 1978. The following year, when manager Bobby Saxton left St James Park to take over the hot seat at Plymouth, he paid a £22,000 transfer fee for John.

As the Pilgrims languished in the Third Division, John became an automatic choice for the next four seasons. He proved to be an able and selfless leader of the attack, where his goals-to-games ratio did not accurately reflect his overall contribution to the team. His chance to play for a third Devon club came in August 1983, when he arrived at Plainmoor and made 30 League appearances, before moving once again to Exeter. His arrival did not save the Grecians from propping up the table and having to apply for re-election to save their League status.

Mine host, John Sims, at his Torquay pub.

Torquay were entering a similarly bleak period in their history. Former Chelsea star Dave Webb had bought control of the club, and allowed John to move to their Devon rivals for financial reasons. He brought him back to Plainmoor nine months later, but the striker's displays could not prevent United from suffering the same fate as Exeter, as they finished at the foot of the Fourth Division. Next season, the team fared no better, and Webb handed over control of team matters to John, who had started the season as reserve team coach. United suffered 6 defeats in 7 League games under their new manager, before he was cruelly relieved of his post – after only a month in charge. It was enough to drive anyone to drink, and John quit the game to become a publican.

Club	Played	Appearances			Goals		
		League	*FAC*	*FLC*	*League*	*FAC*	*FLC*
City	*1978-84*	59	2	2	17	1	1
Argyle	*1979-83*	163	11	8	43	3	2
United	*1983-85*	47	1	4	11	0	1
Total		269	14	14	71	4	4

Peter Whiston signs for United.

PETER WHISTON (DEFENDER)
born Widnes 4 January 1968

Defender Peter Whiston was a trainee electronics engineer at Devonport before signing as a professional for Argyle, shortly before his twentieth birthday. Failing to win a regular place in the first team, he was given a free transfer, and joined up with former Argyle manager Dave Smith at Torquay in March 1990. The following season, his form at right-back was a revelation, as the Gulls stormed to the top of the Fourth Division. Unfortunately, injury interrupted his progress, and robbed him of a place in the starting line-up for United's victory over Blackpool in the play-off final at Wembley.

United's tenure in the Third Division was short-lived and, as they headed straight back to the soccer basement, Peter left for Exeter in an exchange deal that brought Darren Rowbotham to Plainmoor. Therefore, both players simultaneously moved to play for their third Devon club, and faced each other a month later, when Exeter defeated their derby rivals in the preliminary round of the Autoglass Trophy.

Peter's outstanding displays as a central defender impressed Exeter manager Alan Ball. When the former member of England's 1966 World Cup-winning team took over the reins of Premiership side Southampton, he returned to his former club and paid £30,000 in August 1994 to take Peter to the South Coast. The transfer resulted in only one substitute appearance in the top flight, before a final £50,000 move to Shrewsbury, and an appearance in the 1996 Auto Windscreen Shield final at Wembley. His League career ended disappointingly in 1997, after a season where he missed numerous games through injury, and suffered a dubious hat-trick of sending-offs through a series of highly-questionable refereeing decisions. Moving to non-League Stafford Rangers, Peter also took a job outside soccer as a financial consultant in his hometown of Widnes.

		Devon Club Appearances			Goals		
Club	Played	League	FAC	FLC	League	FAC	FLC
Argyle	1987-90	10	1	0	0	0	0
United	1990-91	40	1	5	1	0	1
City	1991-93	85	10	7	7	0	0
Total		*135*	*12*	*12*	*8*	*0*	*1*

DARREN ROWBOTHAM
(FORWARD)
born Cardiff 22 October 1966

Former Welsh Youth team captain, Darren Rowbotham, joined Plymouth in November 1984 on the Youth Training Scheme. He was in the squad that won promotion to the Second Division but he failed to gain a regular place in the side. When he moved on to Exeter in October 1987, half of his 50 senior appearances for Argyle had been made as substitute.

The striker hit his goal-scoring rhythm with City, and was the club's top marksman in 1989 and 1990. On the latter occasion, his 20 goals in 31 League games did much to ensure that Exeter were promoted as champions of the Fourth Division. The celebrations were tempered by the fact that Darren missed the run-in at the end of the season, when he incurred a serious knee injury.

Darren Rowbotham relaxing at Plainmoor.

After a lengthy lay-off, Darren struggled to regain his best form. In September 1991, he moved to Torquay in an exchange deal which took Peter Whiston in the opposite direction. His stay with United was brief. He re-discovered the goal-scoring knack, as his travels took him to Birmingham City, Mansfield, Hereford and Crewe, before he rejoined Exeter in 1996. Back at St James Park, he won a hat-trick of consecutive Player of the Year awards and was granted a benefit year in 1999. He celebrated in style by chalking up his 100th goal for the Grecians, before bidding farewell to the fans at the Park in a testimonial game against West Ham in July 2000.

| Club | Played | Devon Club Appearances | | | Goals | | |
		League	FAC	FLC	League	FAC	FLC
Argyle	1984-87	46	3	1	2	1	0
City	1987-00	235	16	15	86	9	6
United	1991-92	14	3	0	3	0	0
Total		295	22	16	91	10	6

Dave Walters – didn't give up his day job on the farm.

DAVE WALTER
(GOALKEEPER)
born Holsworthy 3 September 1964

Goalkeeper Dave Walter played for all three Devon clubs in a League career which spanned only four years. Signed by Exeter from Bideford in November 1988, he had the dubious distinction of becoming the first City custodian to be sent off, under the new law introduced to combat the so-called 'professional foul'. He got his marching orders after bringing down an onrushing forward, in the home win over Peterborough in April 1989.

Dave won a championship medal the following season, as City topped the Fourth Division under manager Terry Cooper. This success was tempered by the disappointment of relinquishing the keeper's jersey to Kevin Miller during the latter half of the campaign. Following a loan period at Plymouth, Dave made a permanent move to Home Park, where he was understudy for two seasons to first-choice 'keeper Rhys Wilmot.

Moving to Torquay in June 1992, Dave's League career came to an end after only one appearance, conceding four goals in the opening match of the season against Crewe Alexandra. He was dropped, and his part-time contract terminated, after only six weeks at Plainmoor. Having turned full-time professional at the relatively late age of twenty-four, Dave combined his soccer career with running a sheep farm he owned, near Holsworthy. United manager Paul Compton told the *Herald Express*: 'The travelling seems to have been getting Dave down and he feels that he's lost a bit of his appetite for the game'.

		Devon Club Appearances		
Club	*Played*	*League*	*FAC*	*FLC*
City	1988-90	44	2	7
Argyle	1990-92	15	2	0
United	1992	1	0	0
Total		60	4	7

RUSSELL COUGHLIN
(MIDFIELD)
born Swansea 15 February 1960

Midfield player Russell Coughlin had been a Manchester City apprentice, and won promotion honours with Blackburn Rovers and Carlisle United, before joining his first Devon club in July 1984. He was signed by Argyle, and the following season missed only one League game, as the Pilgrims gained promotion by finishing runners-up in the Third Division.

After making over 150 appearances for Argyle, Russell moved on to Blackpool, his home town (Swansea) and Shrewsbury, before returning to end his League career in Devon. The veteran midfield battler spent consecutive seasons with teams that finished at the bottom of the League, yet miraculously avoided the 'big drop'.

Russell Coughlin – twice avoided the 'big drop'.

Signing for Exeter, Russell found himself in the side propping up the League at the end of the 1994/95 season. The Grecians received an amazing reprieve, when the Conference Champions, Macclesfield Town's, ground was deemed unsuitable by the Football League. Likewise, the following season, when Russell joined Torquay, the Gulls finished eleven points adrift at the foot of the table. They too clung onto their League status, when their designated replacement, Stevenage Borough, were also excluded by ground regulations. This decision was upheld by the High Court, when the anguished non-League club issued a writ against the Football League. After these tortuous campaigns, thirty-six-year-old Russell called it a day. Following spells with non-League Dorchester Town and Gretna, he settled in Carlisle.

| Club | Played | Devon Club Appearances | | | Goals | | |
		League	FAC	FLC	League	FAC	FLC
Argyle	1984-87	131	8	8	18	1	2
City	1993-95	68	5	1	0	0	0
United	1995-96	25	3	0	0	0	0
Total		224	16	9	18	1	2

Exeter's Chris Curran in a League match at Plainmoor in February 2000.

CHRIS CURRAN (DEFENDER)
born Birmingham 17 September 1971

Midlands-born Chris Curran has spent all his playing career with either Torquay, Exeter or Plymouth. In February 2000, it was announced that, in recognition of ten years' service to Devon clubs, a benefit year had been awarded. The event was launched in a blaze of publicity at former world Formula One racing champion, Nigel Mansell's, Woodbury Park Golf and Country Club.

Taken on as a trainee by Torquay, the versatile defender made over 150 appearances for the Gulls. He was a member of the team that won promotion on a memorable night at Wembley, when they won the Fourth Division play-off final against Blackpool in 1991. In December 1995, Plymouth paid their neighbours £40,000 to take Chris to Home Park. Six months later, Chris was back at Wembley, as the Pilgrims repeated United's success defeating Darlington to win promotion to Division Two.

Chris proved his worth playing anywhere in defence or midfield, but settled at centreback, following his £20,000 transfer to Exeter in July 1997. A cruciate ligament injury resulted in a lengthy lay-off, but once fully recovered, his combative qualities at the heart of the Grecians' defence have been invaluable over the past few seasons. During the Millennium season, it seemed possible that he would become the first player to represent all three Devon clubs at Wembley. Unfortunately, Exeter fell at the last hurdle, losing to Bristol City in the two-leg semi-final of the Auto Windscreens Shield. This left the Grecians as one of the few current League clubs never to have achieved the honour of playing at Wembley.

		Devon Club Appearances			Goals		
Club	Played	League	FAC	FLC	League	FAC	FLC
United	1990-95	152	8	15	4	0	0
Argyle	1995-97	30	1	1	0	0	0
City	1997-	81	6	4	5	0	0
Total		263	15	20	9	0	0

KEN VEYSEY (GOALKEEPER)
born Hackney 8 June 1967

In 1999, goalkeeper Ken Veysey became the latest player to appear for all three Devon clubs, when he was rescued from non-League football, not for the first time, by manager Kevin Hodges.

Ken made his League debut for Torquay, after being signed from Dawlish in November 1987. After a century of games, he lost his place to Gareth Howells and moved on to Oxford in October 1990. Three years later, he was on Reading's books as a non-contract player, when he returned to Devon and made a handful of appearances for Exeter, and then played in the 1994 Devon Bowl final for Plymouth, before joining non-League Dorchester Town.

His League career appeared to be over, but he was offered another opportunity by

In safe hands! Ken Veysey cradles his daughter Georgina in September 1998.

Torquay chief Kevin Hodges. The former Argyle favourite led a resurgent United to the brink of promotion in 1998. The Gulls went into the final match of the season at Leyton Orient, needing only a draw to ensure them automatic promotion to Division Two. United lost, and Ken was sent off for a professional foul. The resultant suspension meant that he was cruelly denied a place in the play-off final, where Torquay lost to Colchester. Nine years earlier, injury had unluckily robbed him of another Wembley appearance for the Gulls in the Sherpa Van Trophy final against Bolton.

Further disappointment followed when he was not retained the following season, after Kevin Hodge had moved to take charge at Home Park. However, Ken bounced back to League soccer yet again, when his former boss signed him for Argyle, as cover for first-choice 'keeper Jon Sheffield. When called upon, he never let the side down, but was released by the club in May 2000.

	Devon Club *Appearances*			
Club	*Played*	*League*	*FAC*	*FLC*
United	*1987-97*	*110*	*14*	*3*
City	*1993-94*	*12*	*0*	*0*
Argyle	*1999-00*	*6*	*2*	*1*
Total		*128*	*16*	*4*

Ellis Stuttard during his playing days at Plainmoor.

ELLIS STUTTARD

If the twelve post-war players that have played for all three Devon clubs could have been assembled as a squad at one moment in time, then the late Ellis Stuttard would have been uniquely qualified to be become general manager. During an association with Devon clubs, which spanned five decades, he played for Plymouth and Torquay, before serving Plymouth and Exeter in various backroom capacities, including the managerial 'hot seat'.

Ellis joined Plymouth in 1938, but made only one first-team appearance before war intervened. Upon resuming his career, he was transferred to Torquay in 1947. After four seasons at Plainmoor, the defender was awarded a benefit match, and turned out for United against Argyle Reserves at Home Park in May 1952, before moving to non-League Bideford. The job of assistant manager at Swindon Town prepared him for a chequered career in management with Devon clubs. After a spell at Home Park as assistant trainer, he took charge of team affairs in November 1961, but two seasons later dropped down to number two, under Andy Beattie. Arriving at St James Park as chief scout in December 1965, he was appointed manager a month later, when Jack Edwards resigned. The following season, the Grecians were relegated and the ever-jovial Ellis returned to Home Park as chief scout. He became manager in 1970, reverted to chief scout two years later, and remained with Argyle, filling numerous posts until being made redundant in 1982. Retiring to his home town of Burnley, Ellis passed away two years later, but is still remembered with affection by an older generation of Devon soccer fans

JACK EDWARDS

When Crystal Palace full-back Jack Edwards cleared a shot off the line to deny Torquay victory, and thus rob them of the championship of the Third Division (South) in the last game of the 1956/57 season, he could little have realised that he would one day manage the Devon club. In fact, he remains the only man to serve on the management teams of Torquay, Exeter and Plymouth.

When his playing days were over, Jack joined Exeter as trainer, and when he stepped up to management, Jack enjoyed spectacular success by leading the Grecians to their first-ever promotion campaign in 1964. Internal squabbles

Crystal Palace full-back Jack Edwards (right) shadows Torquay's Sam Collins in a crucial League game in May 1957.

saw him leave the following season, when the board appointed Ellis Stuttard as chief scout, without bothering to inform their manager! Joining Torquay as chief scout, he was appointed coach when Frank O'Farrell took charge in 1965. The partnership worked wonders, and United immediately won promotion.

Jack became club manager in 1971, then returned to Exeter two years later as trainer. When manager John Newman left for Grimsby in December 1976, Jack took over as caretaker-manager, until Bobby Saxton was installed as player-manager. At the end of the season, the pair had guided the Grecians to promotion. When former Argyle skipper Saxton accepted an offer to replace Malcolm Allison at Plymouth in 1979, Jack accompanied him to Home Park as coach. The new team showed promise, until Bobby Saxton accepted the chance of taking over from Howard Kendall at Blackburn Rovers in 1981. Jack stayed on at Home Park to coach the reserves under Bobby Moncur, as he completed a twenty-year connection with Devon League clubs.

GEORGE GILLIN

George Gillin – the grand old man of Devon soccer.

Hotelier George Gillin's association with Devon football began in 1932 and lasted sixty-six years. He sat, at various times, on the boards of all three Devon clubs, was chairman of Torquay and Exeter and, towards the end of his distinguished life in football administration, served terms as president of both Plymouth and Torquay.

Joining the Argyle board during the Depression, his premises were bombed during the Blitz, and thereafter, he concentrated his business operations in Torquay. Vice-chairman of United in the aftermath of the Second World War, George was instrumental in obtaining the club's greatest player in 1949. A personal friend, who also happened to be chairman of QPR, arranged for Ranger's inside forward Don Mills to move to South Devon on loan.

Taking over as United chairman in 1950, George resigned four years later, on a matter of principle about the way his fellow directors had conducted the transfer of Harry Parfitt to Cardiff. Switching his allegiance to Exeter until 1957, he then returned to Plymouth for a year, until Ron Blindell swept in with a new board. Rejoining City until 1966, his stay included spells as vice-chairman and chairman. George was particularly proud of his involvement in signing striker Alan Banks to boost the team's successful promotion bid in 1964.

The 'Grand Old Man of Devon Soccer' was installed as president of Argyle in 1968, and held this office until a similar honour was bestowed on him by Torquay. In this capacity, George celebrated his eighty-fifth birthday during the Gull's Golden Jubilee year in 1977. Stepping down in 1988, George was appointed a Life Patron of Torquay United, but sadly did not live to see them become the first Devon club to reach Wembley a year later.

United chairman Mike Bateson being kissed by Dan McCauley!

DAN MCCAULEY

In his autobiography, *Clown Prince of Soccer*, England international Len Shackleton famously donated a blank page to a chapter entitled 'The average director's knowledge of football'. Yet, loathe 'em or hate 'em, Devon clubs would certainly have folded long ago without a succession of local businessmen willing to dig deep into their pockets to keep the clubs afloat.

Boardroom wrangles can often relieve the tedium when there is little for fans to cheer on the pitch and Bampton businessman Dan McCauley certainly did not win any popularity contests in his quest to own a Devon club. Despite arranging for a £100,000 cheque to be delivered to St James Park, his attempts to win support for his bid to take over Exeter City by floating additional shares failed. He was eventually removed from the board by his fellow directors in 1986. Joining the board of Torquay, Dan's company, Rotolok, sponsored the club's first-team strip, before he walked out believing that his financial input should have given him more say in the decision-making. Turning his attention to Plymouth Argyle, he took control during the 1991/92 season. The million-aire's bold promises failed to save the club from free-falling from the old Second to the Third Division. A Wembley play-off victory signalled a temporary recovery, before rele-gation reunited Plymouth with Exeter and Torquay in Division Three.

Argyle's much-maligned supremo had a rollercoaster ride, before accepting an offer from a consortium to sell his interest in the club on the eve of the 2001/2002 season. While his severest critics applauded this move, other fans acknowledged the point that his financial input had kept the club viable. As a newspaperman commented soon after Dan took over at Home Park: 'Heaven help them if he ever loses his wallet'.

STATISTICS
Devon Players of the Year

Year	Plymouth Argyle	Exeter City	Torquay United
1965	-	Arnold Mitchell	-
1966	John Newman	Keith Harvey	-
1967	Norman Piper	Jimmy Blain	-
1968	Pat Dunne	Cecil Smyth	-
1969	David Burnside	Alan Banks	Andy Donnelly
1970	Derek Ricard	Graham Parker	Alan Welsh
1971	Jim Furnell	Campbell Crawford	Dick Edwards
1972	Dave Provan	Jimmy Giles	Dick Edwards
1973	Neil Hague	Jimmy Giles	Mike Mahoney
1974	Ernie Machin	Fred Binney	Mike Mahoney
1975	Paul Mariner	Jimmy Giles	Dave Stocks
1976	Paul Mariner	Peter Hatch	Pat Cruse
1977	Neil Ramsbottom	Peter Hatch	Clint Boulton
1978	George Foster	John Hore	Ian Twitchin
1979	Fred Binney	Colin Randell	John Turner
1980	George Foster	John Delve	Steve Cooper
1981	David Kemp	Tony Kellow	Peter Coffill
1982	John Sims	George Foster	Brian Wilson
1983	Gordon Nisbet	Keith Viney	Colin Anderson
1984	Gordon Staniforth	Keith Viney	Colin Anderson
1985	Tommy Tynan	Ray Pratt	Kenny Allen
1986	Kevin Hodges	Steve Harrower	Derek Dawkins
1987	Tommy Tynan	Tony Kellow	Tom Kelly
1988	Tommy Tynan	Paul Batty	Jim McNichol
1989	Tommy Tynan	Steve Neville	Ken Veysey
1990	Nicky Marker	Shaun Taylor	Phil Lloyd
1991	Kenny Brown	Kevin Miller	Wes Saunders
1992	Dwight Marshall	Peter Whiston	Paul Holmes
1993	Steve McCall	Kevin Miller	Darren Moore
1994	Steve McCall	Peter Fox	Paul Trollope
1995	Craig Skinner	Peter Fox	Lee Barrow
1996	Mick Heathcote	Darren Rowbotham	Charlie Oatway
1997	Chris Billy	Darren Rowbotham	Alex Watson
1998	Martin Barlow and Carlo Corazzin	Darren Rowbotham	Jon Gittens
1999	Mick Heathcote	Ashley Bayes	Neville Southall
2000	Paul McGregor	Garry Alexander	Kevin Hill
2001	Wayne O'Sullivan	Jamie Campbell	Jimmy Aggrey